The Skinny

THE SKINNY

MY MESSY, HOPEFUL FIGHT FOR FULL RECOVERY FROM ANOREXIA

SHERI SEGAL GLICK

Toronto, 2023

RE: Books

www.rebooks.ca

Published in Canada by RE: Books.

ADDRESS:
re:books
380 Macpherson Ave. Suite 306
Toronto ON
M4V 3E3
www.rebooks.ca

First RE: Books Edition: June 2023

ISBN: 978-1-7386702-4-6
eBook ISBN: 978-1-7386702-5-3

Library and Archives Canada Cataloguing in Publication
Title: The skinny : my messy, hopeful fight for full recovery from anorexia / Sheri Segal Glick.
Names: Segal Glick, Sheri, author.
Identifiers: Canadiana (print) 2023015171X |
Canadiana (ebook) 20230151817 | ISBN 9781738670246 (softcover) | ISBN 9781738670253 (EPUB)
Subjects: LCSH: Segal Glick, Sheri—Health. |
LCSH: Anorexia nervosa—Patients—Biography. |
LCGFT: Autobiographies.
Classification: LCC RC552.A5 S44 2023 |
DDC 616.85/2620092—dc23
Printed and bound in Canada.
1 3 5 7 9 10 8 6 4 2

Cover design by: Elspeth Tory

*For my children, who changed my life
in all of the best ways.*

A QUICK NOTE

Thank you for contemplating reading my book. I'm so excited!

Before you start (or don't, whatever, it's cool) I want to get a couple of things out of the way.

This is my story (I'd say journey, but that makes me want to gag, so I can't). My experience of anorexia has been very typical: I got very thin when I was very ill, people noticed, and I was hospitalized. Though this is how many people imagine anorexia, and how it's generally portrayed in the media, recent studies show that more people suffer from restrictive eating disorders, including anorexia, in bigger bodies than in small, emaciated ones (bodies react very differently to starvation). And thanks to misleading stereotypes, it's harder for those members of the population to be taken seriously and get access to care. But that's not my story; this one is, so this is what I wrote about. I can't emphasize enough that you can't tell by looking at someone whether they're healthy or not. I've struggled just as much in my healthy-looking body as I did in my emaciated one, and people in fat bodies can be suffering with very severe anorexia. Eating disorders are mental illnesses.

I wrote this book over the course of my recovery effort. There are things I feel and think at the beginning that I happily don't feel or think in later chapters, or now. I believe that it's valuable to keep those pieces intact because if you are a friend or a parent of someone going through recovery, or someone who has anorexia, or even if you are someone who has engaged in chronic dieting, it's important to see that our thoughts change in recovery with neural rewiring and well ... more calories. Brains are exceptionally cool and amazing.

So, just like I've resisted the urge to go back and fix all of the poetry I wrote in high school, I've resisted the urge to change anything I wrote—even where those thoughts and feelings have changed drastically—because it reflects how I felt, and I think it's crucial to see how much things can change, even when we're sure they can't.

I'll also add that the stories and details are being recounted through the lens of my memory and perception (sorry, I know this is obvious, but I went to law school and one doesn't come out without a few tics).

Finally, although I've kept most people's real names, I have two close friends named Kirsten and Kiersten respectively (Kirsten/Kierstens are the actual best and everyone should have at least one, and I feel truly terrible for anyone who has none). As such, for the purpose of not confusing the crap out of everyone, I've changed Kiersten's name to Cali, which is her dog's name, but Cali is the best girl ever, so it makes sense to me.

Okay. That's it. Thank you for reading this far!

CHAPTER 1

I'm trying to think of funny stuff to say about recovering from anorexia. The things I frequently write about the subject are so earnest and sad, and if there's one thing I care about as much as being thin (or not-fat), it's being funny. In fact, I think I care more about funny. I wouldn't give up funniness for a life of promised-thinness. But I might give it up to avoid a life of promised-fatness. And that's recovery in a nutshell. A tedious and never-ending game of *Would You Rather*.

Would you rather be tormented and thin or free and possibly fat? Would you rather give up every behavior that makes you feel safe and in control knowing that it's the only way that you might *ever* be truly safe and in control? Would you rather feel horrible today so that you can feel better at some point in the future? Would you rather swim in a pool of human snot or dog poop?

Being quasi-recovered also changes the calculus. Because life is so much better than it used to be, or could be. It's your abusive partner who doesn't hit you anymore but still calls you horrible names. When you're acutely ill, there comes a point when you are so sick of dragging your tired body around, and hearing your heart beat in your chest, and being so cold you hurt, and being so consumed with self-loathing, that there is no game of *Would You Rather* without the word "die" at the end. But coming from a place of semi or quasi-recovery, it's pretty easy to find yourself wondering what's the harm in a little obsession in exchange for a life of slim-and-coping?

And then one day it hits you, *maybe*. Maybe you slip and lose a few pounds too many. Maybe you realize that the exercise isn't a source of stress relief, but that you're actually terrified not to do it, and now relief comes only in short bursts before the terror builds up again. Maybe you think you'd like to be able to go out for dinner with friends without having to work on a six-page list of excuses for why you aren't eating (parasite only works so many times, and Ebola works only once).

You worry that your kids might notice that you meticulously measure your cereal and milk before you eat it, or you get a tibial fracture while out running with a friend because your bone density is that bad.

Maybe none of it, or maybe, all of it.

Maybe you decide that you would rather leap into the dog poop, because you've spent far too long swimming in the snot.

CHAPTER 2

My eating disorder started somewhere between grade six and grade seven. I went from spending my allowance money on clothes for my Cabbage Patch Dolls to spending it on diet pills over the course of about a year. (Wait! Do I sound younger if I say that I went from spending my allowance on leg warmers to Jane Fonda workout videos?)

I grew up the eldest of three in a looks and weight-obsessed family. My sister and brother were tiny little waif-like things, and I was a normal-sized kid who liked eating cream cheese by the slice. It was very important to my parents that I not get fat, so when I got a little chubby toward the end of the fourth grade, they said helpful things like how pretty I could look if I lost a few pounds and that if I had stayed at sleepaway camp a little longer, I could have come home looking like a model (I lost weight because I was homesick. Also, yes, the homesickness is a little confusing to me too).

The summer before grade six my mother told me that I only looked fat from the front (great news!) as my back, legs, and arms were still slim. She decided the way to make me slim all over would be to limit my sweets and candy intake to one treat a day. This would have probably been okay if I were a middle-aged woman with no access to Spanx, or if my mom was a professional I was paying for weight loss tips, but as I was an eleven-year-old who loved candy and had no real concept of what bodies should or shouldn't look like, it was not the best.

I remember calling my mom from my friend Lisa's olive-green kitchen phone and asking if I could have a saltwater taffy with Lisa and her older brother Shawn. My mom replied that I should picture "skinny little Lisa in her bathing suit," and then picture myself, and decide. Hanging up the phone, I looked Lisa in the eye and said, "My mom said yes." Though I also remember eating that taffy and, for the first time, feeling what I would later learn to identify as guilt. It was my Garden of Eden moment, I guess.

Much to my mother's disappointment, her summer weight-loss plan didn't work. Maybe I was a little disappointed too. For the first day of grade six I chose a mini skirt to accentuate my not-fat legs and a baggy sweater to hide my not-thin stomach. I didn't have any real concept of my body shape, other than what my mother had told me, but I knew enough to know that I was less cute and lovable than my tiny siblings.

CHAPTER 3

The term "perfect storm" isn't meant to describe happy things (*it was the perfect storm of low humidity, a fresh haircut, and a new conditioner that contributed to that amazing hair day!*). Rather, it's used when a confluence of factors creates a particularly bad situation, like a forest fire, or a street riot, or … an unusually severe storm.

Anorexia is a perfect storm. You need warm moist air (you are sensitive, a perfectionist, a pleaser), cool and dry air from a high-pressure system (the genetics), and tropical moisture (you go into energy deficit as a result of caloric restriction). Lightning.

Diets don't work for most people because they make them feel like crap. But if you have the genetics for anorexia and you go on a diet, everything feels calmer, easier, less important. You have found your drug.

Everything came together for me in the winter of grade six. It was one off-the-cuff comment about my body, made by a client of my dad's on a winter trip to Grenada, that for whatever reason sliced me to the core. To my parents' shock (what's going on? Can she *hear us* when we say mean things about her body?!), I ran out of the room crying. The next day I skipped breakfast. And asked my mom what was more fattening—breakfast or a Snickers bar (answer: "I don't know, Sheri. Both").

The first things I gave up were sweets and pastries. Then fried food. Then snacks (and eventually meat, bread, and all foods that weren't water or NutraSweet-based). My parents were really proud of my "incredible self-control" (they would probably be less impressed had they known how easy it all was. No one tell them, okay?). They started complimenting me on my appearance "your dad thinks that you're his most beautiful child" (not weird at all) and seemed to be prouder of my weight loss than anything I had ever done (which is cool, straight As are meaningless without a thigh gap).

Not eating made me feel special, for a while. My friends noticed I'd stopped bringing lunch to school and frequently expressed concern, which I remember resenting and appreciating. My mom, however, was still bursting with pride over my new disordered lifestyle choices, even telling my teacher at grade eight meet-the-teacher night that I was excellent at math because I was always counting calories. (Note: this remains true to this day. That said, a fancy calculator is probably just as effective and less disruptive than thirty-plus years of anorexia.)

I keep trying to remember when I made my last choice before the illness took hold. Or if any of the choices were mine. Was I trying to lose weight when I started buying appetite suppressants? Did I think that I was fat? How? (Note to pharmacists: twelve-year-olds should not be buying appetite suppressants, even if they are wearing blue eye shadow and look super-sophisticated.) I do know this: once I went into energy deficit, I was no longer controlling any of it; anorexia was.

CHAPTER 4

Finding out you still have an eating disorder years after you thought you had recovered is similar to finding out you're pregnant. All of a sudden you understand why you don't feel like eating much of the time and why you aren't comfortable in your body. You understand why you have weird food aversions and/or digestive issues and why you're always cold (or hot, in the case of pregnancy). You are perhaps in shock and maybe need an adjustment period. You understand why you aren't *getting* a period. Maybe you are afraid. Or maybe you are in denial and give birth at your prom.

I know it seems like a weird thing not to know that you have an eating disorder, particularly if you spent many years being treated for one. But there's this thing called anosognosia, which is a symptom of mental illness that impairs a person's ability to perceive his or her mental illness (*amazing*, right?). That's why some people with anorexia don't know that they're ill. In my case, I knew that I *had* been ill, but I was also pretty sure that I was *no longer* ill. I was eating something other than vegetables, diet popsicles, and diet coke, I wasn't spending four hours a day at the gym, and I ate carbs! And candy! And really, do people with anorexia eat chocolate? (Yes, sometimes.)

Once in a while, I'd have a pang of is-this-normal? Not when I secretly slid food off my plate and onto my husband's at dinner parties when the hosts weren't looking, or when I couldn't eat lunch until after my cleaner left because I didn't want her to see me measuring my yogurt, or when I couldn't eat my wedding cake, or when I needed drugs to ovulate in order to get pregnant because I didn't get a period. Not those times. Though after the birth of my first child, who had been born perfect but tiny (#humblebrag), I was plagued by the idea that it had been my fault he was so small. I worried that I should have gained more weight while I was pregnant, or exercised less, or eaten more dietary fat. I even went so far as to Google articles about recovered anorexics who give birth to small children (*I know!*). But really, aside from that one moment of almost-clarity, I was pretty confident that I was fine, and I went on to have a second tiny baby two years later.

Then came my third pregnancy. This one felt different because I stopped getting hungry. I was able to force myself to eat because I knew that I couldn't starve my unborn child (motherhood really does bring out the best in people!) but I spent much of that time riddled with anxiety given how guilty and uncomfortable I felt eating without an appetite. After I gave birth, my hunger cues came back, but then, about nine months after my daughter was born, they stopped again and I was paralyzed by fear at every meal, anticipating the post-eating distress I'd become so accustomed to during my pregnancy.

Eventually, I went to the doctor and told her I'd lost the desire to eat. She ordered blood tests. They couldn't find anything wrong. More tests. They still couldn't find anything wrong. The unsettled feeling that I was unwell but not knowing why went on for over a year. I was frequently stressed, had a shorter fuse than usual, couldn't sleep, had pelvic floor issues (I'm not going to elaborate), and, of course, no hunger cues.

I forced myself to eat, but it wasn't enough, and I lost weight. Because I was breastfeeding a baby, and running after two other little kids, the ten or so pounds I initially lost were easy to explain to anyone who noticed. And then one day, I got on the scale, and the red flashing number was one that I hadn't seen as an adult. I felt fear-elation.

Sensing the elation part was not a good thing, I made an appointment with a psychologist. The wait to see her was about eight months, and by the time my name came up, I'd started to get hungry again and my eating was mostly back to me-normal. But I still went to the appointment.

Psychologist:	What brings you here today?
Me:	First of all, I basically made this appointment in the 1980s. Do you have any idea how long your waitlist is? What if I was really sick? I mean, I'm not, but I'm sure there are a lot of people who really need help. It's very bad.
Psychologist:	Yes, my waitlist is long. Thanks for sticking it out. What brings you here today?
Me:	When I initially made this appointment ... *eight months ago* ... I had no appetite and I couldn't eat, and then one day I weighed myself and realized that I'd lost more weight than I'd noticed ... which I guess makes sense because I couldn't keep any of my pants up without rolling them at the waist. Anyway, my hunger cues are pretty much back to normal, so that's good news, because as long as I have hunger cues, I can eat.
Psychologist:	You can't eat when you're not hungry?
Me:	No.
Psychologist:	What if it's a mealtime?
Me:	No.

Psychologist:	I'm glad you're here. Tell me more about that.
Me:	Meh. Not much to tell, I feel guilty and stressed if I eat when I'm not physically hungry, so I don't really do it. It might be a remnant from when I had anorexia.
Psychologist:	Tell me about the anorexia.
Me:	I was very ill when I was a teenager but then I decided that I didn't want to be in and out of the hospital for the rest of my life. I started eating more and my weight went up, and now—as long as I'm hungry—I eat three meals every day. I'm basically all better.
Psychologist:	If you're all better, why did you come today?
Me:	I have little kids and I know that there's a genetic component to eating disorders. I want to get rid of some of my lingering behaviors so that I can set a good example.
Psychologist:	What are some of the behaviors you're worried about?
Me:	Well, I can't eat anything unless I know the exact calorie count which means that I have to weigh and measure everything, and I can't eat at people's houses or in restaurants, and I'm terrified of oil in my food. And I sometimes feel crushing guilt after I eat.
Psychologist:	Is that it?
Me:	Mostly. I also exercise quite a bit every day and feel like I have to walk everywhere. Anyway … if we could fix those few things, that would be helpful.
Psychologist:	Those are symptoms of your anorexia.

Me: I don't have anorexia.

Psychologist: It's functional anorexia, but it's anorexia. You are still very ill.

Me: No, you're wrong. I've *had* anorexia and I know the difference … this is not that. Also, functional anorexia? Is that an oxymoron?

Psychologist: No, it's what you have.

Me: Well, it sounds ridiculous. Did I tell you that I eat carbs? Do people with anorexia eat carbs?

Psychologist: Yes.

Me: People *without* anorexia also eat carbs. People like me.

Psychologist: Okay. Why are you here?

Me: I told you. To fix the lingering behaviors I have left over from when I *used to have* anorexia.

Psychologist: Okay. Why don't you go home and stop counting calories? Throw out your food scale. Stop exercising for a few days. And then come back and tell me how it went. If you don't have anorexia, you should be able to fix these things pretty easily.

And that's how I found out at the age of forty-four, with my food scale, and running injuries, and osteopenia, and huge mental database of calories, that I still had an eating disorder.

CHAPTER 5

May 8, 2019

<u>To Do</u>

- Stop counting calories
- Eat fear foods
- Eat uncountable things
- Eat until you are full
- Eat when you are hungry
- Eat sometimes when you aren't hungry
- Don't obsess over the uncounted calories
- Don't obsess over the calories in the fear foods
- Don't obsess because you don't know the calories in the uncountable things
- Don't obsess because you ate until you were full, even if it was too much or at the wrong time
- Don't obsess because you ate when you were hungry, even if it was too much or at the wrong time
- Don't obsess because you ate when you weren't hungry
- Stop exercising
- Drive places
- Sit still

- Stop feeling guilty because you haven't exercised
- Stop feeling guilty because you drove
- Stop feeling guilty because you were still
- Stop weighing yourself
- Stop worrying about how much you weigh
- Embrace your new bigger body
- Stop hating yourself for not being able to embrace your new bigger body
- Pretend you are okay with your new bigger body
- Stop hating yourself for pretending to be okay with your new bigger body, even though you actually feel like a disgusting cow
- Stop calling yourself a disgusting cow
- Embrace mindfulness
- Stop hating yourself for not being able to embrace mindfulness because you think it's really hard and boring
- Talk to someone
- Stop feeling guilty and stupid for constantly burdening the person you are talking to
- Don't do the quick fixes, even though they will probably make you feel better
- Know that ultimately the quick fixes won't make you feel that much better
- Do the things that scare you
- Pretend you aren't terrified
- Breathe

CHAPTER 6

I was caught throwing up in the bathroom the night of my grade eight graduation. There had been a ceremony and a dance. All my best friends were there, and I went with a cute guy I really liked (we're now friends on social media, he's still surprisingly cute). I was wearing a white strapless dress with red polka dots and a crinoline underneath, and I remember liking my hair (that might be the first and last time that's ever happened). After the dance, a big group of friends went out for dinner. It all felt very grown-up. I ordered a Caesar salad, ate part of it, and then noticed how creamy the dressing was and how oily the croutons were. How could I have eaten that? How did I let that happen? The happy commotion all around me stopped existing as guilt and panic took hold.

I snuck away to the bathroom and had the bad luck of being in the stall next to some girl in my extended friend group with an anorexic mother (had her mother been an alcoholic, or even someone with a weak gag reflex, it would have gone unnoticed). She accused me of throwing up, I denied it, and by the time I got back to the table, everyone knew, and there was a mini-intervention, as amazingly dramatic and ineffective as one would expect from a group of thirteen-year-olds. I cried and promised that it was the first and last time that I would ever throw up Caesar salad in a white polka dot prom dress and begged my friends not to tell my parents before I left for sleepaway camp. I then made sure they couldn't call my parents by leaving the home phone off the hook until I left for camp four days later. Staying within reach of the phone for ninety-six hours straight was tiring, but worth it. The 1980s were amazing that way.

While I was at camp, one of my friends *did* call my parents. As did the camp (my counselors had noticed that I only ate plain salad and spent most of my free time doing aerobics). When I got back home, now in grade nine, my dad took me to an appointment at the children's hospital. We made small talk in the car on the way, both of us acting like he was taking me to a dental cleaning or an eye exam. I thought he was irritated because he was being forced to take time away from work, because he had such a problem child, but it's possible he was sad or nearly as frightened as I was.

The doctor, who specialized in eating disorders, weighed me and said that if I didn't gain a certain number of pounds (divided into a minimum number per week), I would have to be admitted as an inpatient. Miraculously, I gained nearly all the weight by the next week. In water. My mom has since said that she had asked the doctor if I could have been manipulating my weight in some way, and he had said only by a couple of pounds. I wanted to come up with a punchline to sum all of this up, but I'm not sure I have to. The eating disorder specialist told my parents that I couldn't be manipulating my weight. It made more sense to believe that I'd gained fourteen pounds in seven days (and somehow looked exactly the same).

The thing with grade eight girls and grade nine girls and grade ten girls is that a lot of them are skinny, gangly people, because they are grade eight or grade nine or grade ten girls. So only my closest friends and family knew about my eating disorder. I got a lot of approval for my appearance from peers and weirdly, from adults (teachers, friends' parents, and my mom, who frequently reported back to me which of her friends or their teenage daughters thought I was pretty or—the highest form of compliment she could pay—beautiful). It was a message that I was not only okay, but that I had to keep doing exactly what I was doing. And so I did.

I ate as little as possible and started water-loading two hours before each scheduled weigh-in. There were times I got so sick from all of the water that my vision blurred and my teeth chattered, and it was all I could do to not pee in my pants and throw up while I was being weighed. My incredible ability to drink copious amounts of water and feel like I was going to die, without actually dying, kept me out of the hospital for the next year.

CHAPTER 7

This book doesn't have an end
Said my friend
Which is true
So I should know what to do
I should be able to face all of my stupid petty fears
Without tears
To not calorie count
Or exercise a certain amount
And if my pants don't fit
Fuck it
It shouldn't matter to me,
If I am free
(But it really, really does, which is stupidly frustrating, and
demoralizing and confusing).

CHAPTER 8

My entire reason for this recovery effort is to be more present in my life. To be able to be still with my kids, and accept dinner invitations, and eat at people's houses, and to stop taking frequent and invisible micro-breaks from conversations while I quickly tally up the calories in breakfast-lunch-that-cup-of-coffee-with-two-tablespoons-of-milk-or-was-it-three. The constant, never-ending, Rainman-in-the-casino-style-counting. Re-adding the same numbers to get to the same total, ten, twenty, two hundred times a day.

Being able to count calories with precision means not being able to eat foods that are uncountable, which isn't a big deal. It only means that I can't eat most things at most people's houses, or most things at most restaurants, or most things at most food courts, fairs, sporting events, tourist destinations, or parties. It means I can never eat anything with a sauce or dressing (unless I know the amount used and the caloric value of said sauce or dressing) and without knowing the exact weight (ideally in grams) of all foods prior to eating them. Other than that ... no biggie.

Recently, I've been trying to eat one uncountable thing every day—sometimes it's something terror-inducing, like a premade tuna sandwich (I initially worried that people would find it odd to see a grown woman crying over a sandwich at Whole Foods but was comforted by the thought they'd presume they were tears of shame for realizing that I'm the type of person who spends nine dollars on a tuna sandwich). I have had some scary restaurant meals—not scary in the sense that I was being chased, or sharing a table with a known murderer-rapist, or eating in traffic, but scarier than all of that, because the meals were prepared by someone else and were therefore mostly uncountable. I've stopped using my food scale and, for the most part, my measuring cups. Though the numbers are still there. They're just harder to figure out.

I don't know how to get rid of the numbers. For me, they're like an earworm—a song that gets into your head and you can't make it stop. I had this thought that I would stop calorie counting when I stopped measuring my breakfast cereal. So, after a quick six months of planning, I stopped measuring my morning cereal. For the first week or so I sobbed my way through breakfast (luckily, I'm the first one up in my house). My heart raced like I was being chased by a bear, and I thought I was going to be sick as I shoveled salty (from the tears), unmeasured cereal into my mouth. Eventually—after months of practice—it started to feel blissfully normal. This is all kind of exciting and kind of liberating, but I still attribute the same numbers to it that I was before I stopped measuring (with a ten percent increase, because caloric inflation).

Eight months after I stopped measuring cereal, I gave my food scale to a friend—I had to get it out of the house because no amount of willpower was enough to resist that scale—but the truth is that I'm probably mostly portioning the same amounts that I was without the scale and measuring cups. Eyeballing food and estimating its caloric content with a high degree of precision is one of my super-talents, along with simple math, a huge mental caloric database, the ability to exercise through extreme pain, and the gift of being able to return just about anything to any store.

Restaurant food is harder to eyeball and therefore the scariest thing for me to eat. In restaurants I am forced to accept that I will not have a precise number, and in fact, I might only have a very imprecise number. Eating a restaurant meal also requires physically going to the restaurant, ordering without modifications, and eating what I have ordered. This is only made possible by having a plan, going with a friend that I trust, and ideally being at least a little drunk. Which brings me to wine calories.

Wine consumption is the only thing I'm able to lose track of with some regularity. In the old days, I was very careful to track exactly how much wine I'd had (I would also save calories for wine by not eating, which is apparently not a thing that most people do). And then one day last summer, I lost track. And it was okay. And I've done it since then. Not every time, but enough times that I don't panic when it happens. The truth is that it's kind of amazing to be able to wake up with a terrible headache and not remember how many glasses of wine it took to get to that point. I don't know if I'd feel the same waking up with icing and sprinkles in my hair and not being able to pinpoint how many cupcakes I'd eaten. Though the fact that I can consistently lose track of anything, gives me hope. And also, sometimes, a hangover.

CHAPTER 9

On days that I was being weighed, I skipped my last couple of classes and bought three two-liter bottles of diet soda at the convenience store across the street from the school. I've always found fizzy drinks easier to drink than water, and in those days, I also loved the novel flavor combination of food coloring and NutraSweet. I'd then sit down in a low-traffic area of the school, pull out my large plastic cup, and start drinking diet soda (in retrospect, so, so weird—especially when my friends came to visit between classes).

I'd drink past the point of nausea, past the point of dizziness (and past the point of what was safe—looking back at this now, I can't believe how careless I was with my life and how unbelievably lucky I am that I didn't wind up with brain damage or dead). By the time my dad picked me up for an after-school weigh-in at the children's hospital, my vision would be blurry as a result of water intoxication, and I had to use all of my best acting skills to stand up straight without crying out in pain. And then after getting weighed, I felt more relief than the most tantric-y of tantric sex. Because not only did I avoid hospitalization, I got to pee.

One day, I walked out of the school and found my dad waiting for me (years later, I learned that a couple of friends had told my parents what I was up to). My stomach dropped. I'd been worried about this scenario for as long as I'd been doing weigh-ins—he was there to take me to be weighed without any notice. My head started throbbing. I thought about running, but I had nowhere to go.

The drive was excruciating, and for once not because I had to pee. I was admitted within the hour. Pro: my lifelong dream of having a TV in my bedroom had finally come to fruition. Con: my room was in the hospital, which made all the TV watching decidedly less pleasurable.

I really didn't understand what was happening. I was a fourteen-year-old who had been handed a copy of the *Canadian Mental Health Act* (to be used as a handy reference in case I thought that my rights were being violated, which was hilariously ridiculous because *of course* I did), a menu to fill out (with a seek-a-word and coloring to do on the other side of the page), and a contract to sign.

The contract set out that I would be on forced bed rest and that all personal possessions, including clothing, would be taken away any morning that I failed to gain 100 grams—the weight of two Power Bars or about three cheese strings (uneaten, to be clear). The fact that people with anorexia frequently become hypermetabolic during refeeding was an irrelevant consideration.

What this meant in practical terms was that even if I ate everything placed in front of me, every meal, every snack, some days I wouldn't gain weight. On those days—ones where my confused body needed to use every calorie for repair rather than weight gain—all my belongings would be boxed up, and my bed would frequently be wheeled into the hallway, where I would be forced to spend the day in a hospital gown. Not everyone was wheeled into the hallway, only those of us who'd been caught out of bed (I refused to use a bedpan and was often caught getting up to use the bathroom). While being stuck in bed at the nurses' station was demoralizing and humiliating, the hours of nothing and no one between meals and snacks was the most torturous part. And I was never warm enough in those hospital gowns. It was nothing if not not-motivational.

It took less than a week under the hospital's behavior motivation protocol for my war against my body to metamorphose into a war against the doctors and the nurses. I didn't feel like there was space to be honest or to get better (nor did I understand how to do that). From an inauspicious start (caught with weights inside my underwear! Amateur hour!), I became so good at cheating the system, there were times I left the hospital only a few pounds heavier than when I'd been admitted. My school friends were learning to type (an actual school subject back then) at the same time as I was learning exactly how much water to drink before a weigh-in and how not to involuntarily vomit (because of all the water) immediately after being weighed in case the nurse came back.

The hospital was like a camp-prison. I had an eccentric friend group, made up of regular patients—a handsome bald cancer kid who had recently lost his leg, a couple of kids with cystic fibrosis, and a revolving door of teenage anorexics, all of whom I got to know very well. Once in a while a new kid would be admitted, and they'd join our strange clique—people like superhot-heart-condition-guy (we were caught making out in his room and in a storage closet, and we went on some proper dates once we were both discharged); chronic arthritis girl (she was my roommate and helped me cheat and lie); Spina-bifida girl (she was also my roommate and helped me cheat and lie); and a difficult gum-chomping bulimic (also briefly my roommate, but she was only looking out for herself).

We only had school in the morning; afternoons and evenings were filled with endless downtime. We would steal from supply closets (luxury items like gauze and Band-Aids and surgical tape), wander into the adjoining adult hospital, browse in the gift shop, and on occasion, leave the premises altogether. I also learned to smoke, which gave me another fun and life-enhancing activity to enjoy. If hanging out in the smoking room at age fifteen with three other anorexic teenagers and a cute guy who may or may not be in need of heart surgery isn't the pinnacle of teenage fun and freedom, I don't know what is.

There were psychiatrists who we were assigned to see for about an hour, no more than once a week. Mine was my neighbor, which saved us having to go through any of the weird getting-to-know-you stuff, as I'd already spent some time babysitting his kids. It wasn't awkward at all, and I felt very comfortable telling my parents' friend my secrets. Actually, it was horribly uncomfortable, and we spent a lot of time playing checkers. My only regret is not having spent all that time learning to play chess.

My memories of the hospital are sepia. I remember my heart beating like a marathoner's every time I heard the squeaky scale coming down the hall. I remember crying, misunderstood, frustrated, tears (until I was sure I'd have to drink a bucket of water to compensate for the lost tear-fluid). I remember the stomach cramps caused by the sudden increase of food that gave me goose bumps on translucent skin. Though I also remember the hospital sometimes feeling uncomplicated, and warm, and safe. I remember watching cartoons over breakfast. Laughing with the other girls, who were as heartbroken as I was. Allowing myself as many raisin bran muffins as I wanted. It was a jail-vacation, where everything smelled like industrial cleaner and stale coffee, and for the first time in my life I was surrounded by girls who really understood me, and doctors who really, really didn't. Today, when I find myself at the hospital for an appointment with one of my kids, I get a whiff of that smell, and I'm overwhelmed by feelings of wistfulness for what it was, and for what I wish it had been.

CHAPTER 10

I want to quit recovery today.

I'm sick of listening to all of my friends talk about exercise and feeling like a lazy fraud because I'm trying to do less while they're all trying to do more.

I'm tired of getting compliments on my tiny frame because it's proof that people are paying attention to my body—I worry that when my body changes, everyone will think that I let myself go.

It's ridiculous that I'm forcing myself to eat a brownie, when I'm just as happy with cucumber slices (cucumbers taste more watery and bland, but brownies have an aftertaste of guilt and self-loathing).

Today I don't believe that I will ever be able to eat scary foods without guilt.

Today I don't believe that people will accept me in a bigger body.

Today I don't believe that I will accept me in a bigger body.

Today I don't feel like it's worth it.

Today I don't feel like I'm worth it.

I hope that tomorrow is easier.

CHAPTER 11

I have a long list of foods that I'm afraid of. I'm afraid of them because they're either too calorically dense, or because I can't count the calories in them. Some feel like unnecessary calories (like salad dressing, butter, oil, mayo) because they're things I don't notice missing. But I'm retraining myself to eat these things. And it feels super weird because a lot of people try to avoid these things, and I'm forcing myself to eat them. White flour and refined sugar? Yes please! Frappuccino in lieu of an Americano? Brace yourself, pancreas!

As long as there are foods that still scare me, I won't fully recover. I'm afraid of those foods because I'm afraid of getting fat. And recovery means accepting my body's natural shape. Which sounds like complete bullshit. Because who does that? Do people do that? Kate Moss is famously credited for having said, "nothing tastes as good as skinny feels," and Helen Gurly Brown lived by her mantra "be thin forever; be thin at any price." Of course, Kate was a supermodel, and Helen had a raging eating disorder for most of her adult life. Gurly Brown also admitted to hiding food thrust upon her at parties in friends' couch cushions and suggested this was a workable strategy for dealing with "food pushers." Friends, I would never do that, but I have absolutely hidden food that I'm afraid to eat on my person. You know what feels worse than skinny? Reaching into your pocket and finding smushed cake nestled in a soggy napkin two weeks after a party.

I almost never like anything the first time I try it. The taste of fear is overpowering (butter, oil, sugar, grease, guilt, and terror all taste very similar and can be substituted in any recipe at a ratio of one-to-one). Sometimes I like something the second time, but that's also unusual. It's scary because eating the thing feels tantamount to letting go of the control I have worked so hard to maintain. What if I start loving something so much that I can't stop eating it? What if after three donuts I can't walk by a donut store without buying two every time? What if I have to have a sweet milky coffee whenever I need a caffeine fix? Is coffee even *supposed* to taste good?

When I'm trying something new or scary it ruins everything else that's happening in that moment. I become paralyzed by fear and doubt and guilt. It takes me away from whomever I am with before I eat it, and while I am eating it, and after I eat it, and that feels like total garbage. It feels not worth it.

Then the other week I had theater tickets in another city. My flight was delayed. And delayed again. And when I landed there was a lightning storm. And crazy traffic owing to a big, important sporting event. And the hotel was packed because of the people in town to see the big important sporting event, so I couldn't get an elevator to my room. I was an hour late to meet my friend for dinner. When I arrived at the restaurant my sweet friend nervously told me that she had ordered for us and described what she'd ordered.

Then she asked, "Will you eat that?"

And I was so unbelievably happy and grateful to be able to say yes.

And I did.

And then we went to see the show.

All that practicing paid off.

It was a perfect night.

CHAPTER 12

Fear food list as of today, in order of difficulty. Things with an "x" next to them are foods I've recently eaten, at least once. I've been doing about four per week.

Sweetened/milky coffee drinks (hot) x
Sweetened/milky coffee drink (cold) x
Premade sandwich x
Pasta x
Croissant x
Store-bought muffin, bran x
Cakey muffin x
Donut x
Smoothie x
Scone x
Biscuit x
Gelato x
Ice cream sandwich x
Restaurant breakfast food (French toast or pancakes)
Cookie (packaged with calorie count) x
Ice cream cake x
Wrap x
Restaurant/food stand taco x

Beavertail x
Falafel (no sauce) x
Cookie, not packaged, no calorie count x
Cupcake x
Cake x
Cake with icing
Pastry x
Cinnamon bun x
Ice cream x
Quiche x
Things with melted cheese (not most pizza now though) x
Brownie x
Pie
Falafel (with sauce)
Store-bought Mexican fast food (i.e., Chipotle, Whole Foods, Taco Bell)
Sushi with gross orange mayo slathered on it x
Premade salad with nuts, seeds, quinoa, chickpeas x
Salad with dressing x
Salad with dressing cheese/nuts
"Bowls" s/as:
  – Poke bowl x
  – Burrito bowl
  – Noodle bowl
  – Salad bowl x
Breaded things
Fried fish
French fries x
Thai noodle soup with spicy oil x
All things that come in a sauce, including:
  – Stir fry
  – All Thai food

- All Chinese food
- All Indian food

Macaroni and cheese x

Most Italian food (restaurant pasta, lasagne, etc.)

Movie popcorn

Poutine

CHAPTER 13

Telling people has gotten easier (and if you are currently reading this in book form, apparently much, much easier).

Unlike a few girls I knew in high school who loved talking about their eating disorders, I've always worked hard to keep mine a secret. When I couldn't attend a class trip to France the summer before grade twelve because I couldn't keep my weight up, I told everyone I had mono, even researching symptoms in the library (the *library*! It's hard to even fathom how hard life was before the internet).

If people knew about my eating disorder, we still never talked about it. Even when friends came to visit me in the hospital, no one mentioned the change in surroundings, all of us acting like we expected to see a Benetton or a Swatch store at the end of every hallway (my friends and I spent a lot of time at the mall). We certainly never discussed why I was there.

My eating disorder has always felt like a huge, glaring flaw. Probably because it's a mental illness, and a hole that I haven't been able to pull myself out of. Telling people makes me feel like a weirdo (who in their right mind is afraid of a fried potato? Spoiler: *no one*.); and a failure (I am good at most things but can't figure out *eating*). I worry that it will make me seem needy, or helpless, or broken, all of which I am sometimes.

I've worked so hard for so long to act like I'm normal, it sometimes seems sad to undo all of that hard work (words of a friend upon being told: "Is *this* why we've never gone to Chipotle?!"). I struggle with changing the perceptions of people who only know me as that ultra-together mom who begs her daughter to get up as she lies splayed out screaming in the middle of the sidewalk, no more than ten times a week. In telling someone, I'm exposing my dirtiest secret and my biggest source of shame. It's saying, *You might think that I have things under control, but I don't.*

Telling people also makes me accountable. The more people who know I'm not deathly allergic to all salad dressings, the fewer people there are left to lie to about it when I'm ordering salad. That in itself is scary because then all of us know that I should be eating the dressing and sometimes, I really want to pretend that the issue is with the dressing.

Another thing I worry about is people not believing me. My weight has been sitting somewhere between the high end of underweight and the low end of normal weight for a while now, and I feel like not being emaciated makes the whole thing seem less authentic. Also, people know that I eat pizza! How could they possibly believe me? I presume that no one will understand that recovering from anorexia looks very different from living with anorexia. Recovery involves relearning to do all the things I never did in my eating disorder, like eating more and moving less. It would be easy for an outsider to look at me and think that I'm fine, healthy even. What if they thought the whole thing was made up?

So far, the very short list of people I've told have believed me, and they have amazed me. My friends have supported me in a way that is shocking. And humbling. But it still feels like peeling off a layer of skin every time I tell someone. And I still have an I've-said-too-much-hangover whenever I talk about it, which I'm starting to understand is also part of the illness. Anorexia thrives in secrecy.

My closest friend has confirmed that it does change people's perception of me, but that it's okay because it's better to be the more honest version of myself. And on good days, I believe her.

CHAPTER 14

I'm on a recovery break right now. It's kind of the same as a diet cheat week, but the opposite.

It's pretty stupid. Because either I'm going to do recovery properly, by letting go of my disordered behaviors and gaining as much weight as my body needs, or I'm not. I can lie and say that it's a break to catch my breath, but really, it's to see if I can be happier not-pushing and not-trying. I want to know that I can still lose a pound or two at will, and that I can still run back to anorexia if I want to. Or at least stay here in this place of not-that-ill, but with the knowledge that I am also not well.

My amazing recovery holiday has allowed me to work out every day without guilt (or at least a different brand of guilt from the much more familiar you-didn't-do-enough varietal). I got to skip dinners to make room for wine calories and then got to try my hardest not to get hammered every time I drank on an empty stomach. I was able to wander aimlessly while enjoying the sights at the mall while looking for the lowest-calorie snack option, then triumphantly settle on a dry salad at 10:45 a.m. like a weirdo, or a rabbit. I got to weigh myself daily and feel sweet relief to see the number on the scale go down.

That moment—with the numbers—was supposed to make it all worth it. And now, I'm trying to decide if it did.

It's amazing how quickly old thought patterns came back and how the desire to restrict—if only on a break, for a week or two—bled into everything. It makes all of the recovery things I have done thus far feel simultaneously futile, and urgent.

The other week I met up with an old friend. We live in different cities, and we don't see a ton of each other. We have similar builds and are the same height, and she's always been a generally tiny person with little effort. Last week she told me about a crash diet she went on to get back to the size I am now (her smallest and my biggest). She said she wanted to keep losing weight because she was addicted to the high of seeing the numbers drop. She said she thought it was important for "people like us" (read: shorties) to be thin, and that when "people our size" (the shorties) gain weight, other people notice every extra pound. She also told me she thought I looked great now because I was "not so skinny anymore," but also, that I didn't need to gain any more weight.

I tried to reason with her, telling her about everything she'd be giving up if she kept going and about everything I would be giving up if I stopped here. But her words ignited the dormant crazy centers in my brain. Signs flashing neon pink and green and that awful yellow that no one likes hummed to life, as my friend of twenty years personified my eating disorder voice. And now, I'm questioning whether I'm ready to give up thinness. Because I have never *not* had an eating disorder, I don't know where my weight will land. Maybe I will be thin like my siblings and parents, and maybe I will be a little chubby, like grade-five me, or maybe bigger than that. The not-knowing is terrifying.

Maybe my friend is so caught up in her own stuff that she isn't seeing things clearly. Or maybe she is the only person who is seeing clearly. The only one who is willing to cut through the bullshit and tell me the truth. Packaging matters. And thinness, and the way I look, is mostly what I have to offer.

My friend Kirsten isn't thin. And she's beautiful. Not just beautiful-on-the-inside beautiful (she's that too, which can be unbelievably off-putting when you just want to gossip and talk trash about people in the schoolyard) but also perfect-glowy-skin-with-delicate-features-and-tropical-sea-eyes beautiful. So, when I talk to her about thinness, I presume she's immune. Because she already knows she doesn't need thinness to be pretty or to be an exceptional human. That different rules apply to her. But I got that wrong. And I hurt her feelings when I told her about how my skinny friend got to me. My willingness to believe everything my skinny friend said made my closest friend think I was judging her for the shape of her body, when I was judging myself. I don't feel like I am good enough, or pretty enough, or anything-enough to exist in the world without a thigh gap.

When I think about who I want to be, it's not skinny and obsessed. When I think about the people I love and admire the most, I recognize they're not the thinnest people I know. When I think about how I have felt on this recovery break, I realize it's not happier. I know I need to see this through. That this break has to be a break, and not the end. Though, like any vacation, I'm not quite ready for it to come to an end.

CHAPTER 15

Often I think about stopping here. I've been in recovery for close to a year and sometimes I feel like where I am is good enough. I am in a place where I can eat pizza and drink a latte (from a place where the calorie count is posted). I can skip a workout (under duress). I get regular periods, my bone density has improved, and I can order fish off a menu, drink a cocktail, and lose track of how many glasses of wine I've had. These are things I never expected to be able to do. And many days, it feels like I have come far enough, and as far as I can.

This is all so hard. And it feels unfair and pointless much of the time. There is no guarantee that all of the missed walks and forced salad dressing will pay off.

Stopping here would mean working out most days and never losing the pull to walk as much as I can. It would mean feeling lazy and uncomfortable on days I feel I haven't moved enough. It would mean never knowing what it's like to fully relax—whether at a cottage, or on vacation, or on a sick day. It would mean not easily accepting invitations to eat at people's houses, not being able to eat the meal at my children's weddings, and constantly hoping my kids don't notice that my diet is different from everyone else's.

Stopping here would mean sweet relief. Being able to go back to my food scale and not feeling bad if I just can't use the salad dressing. It would mean saying yes to all of the walks and never again lying in bed at 6 a.m., willing myself not to exercise. It would mean a thigh gap and a flat stomach and comfortably fitting into all of my tiny jeans.

Stopping here could mean a relapse. It could mean being soothed by the seductive voice that tells me everything will feel better if I lose a few pounds, and then a few more. It could mean reverting to walking five hours a day and not being able to eat when I'm not hungry, even if it's the third or fifth day of no appetite. It would mean never knowing what could have been, or watching my children follow in my disordered footsteps and knowing that I broke them.

Maybe I would go back to quasi-recovery and this would all feel like a weird dream.

Or maybe, after the relief started to feel normal again, I might start to wonder what-if. Could things have been different? Did I stop too soon?

And maybe I would try again.

Or maybe, like a dear friend once suggested, I would look back at my life when it was too late and wish I had more time.

And that I hadn't given up.

CHAPTER 16

Have I mentioned there's a voice in my head? It's the voice that calls me fat and worthless and tells me I need to keep walking even when I'm tired, and it's hot, and I passed my house five blocks ago. It's the voice that won't let me finish a bowl of pasta and that forces me to tally up my calories over and over, in case I got the math wrong the first twenty or fifty times.

And the problem with that voice—that mean, critical, unrelenting, voice—is that it sounds exactly like my own. But it's not. It's the voice of my eating disorder.

I don't hear actual voices in my head the way some people do with schizophrenia. The voice is my internal monologue, accompanied by a series of feelings. It's the fear and guilt when I eat something forbidden, or too much, or at the wrong time, or when I'm not hungry. It's when the words "you're so fat" or "you're disgusting" or "you are weak" pop into my head, multiple times a day, out of the blue.

I used to think that it was my voice. For years and years, I thought it was my voice.

It's not. I don't share the same values as my eating disorder. I don't think that people have more or less value because of the shape of their bodies. I don't think that bigger bodies are disgusting. I don't think that people are weak for enjoying food or for eating when they aren't hungry. So, it makes no sense that those things should apply to me.

The voice is how my eating disorder tries to keep me trapped. It hurls all the meanest insults and the most hurtful things. And it has access to the things that hurt the most because it's inside my head. I can't hide because it knows what I've been up to and what will pull me back. It knows all the tricks. It's the worst kind of alarm system.

I fight back by trying to do the opposite of what the voice says to take away its power (this is sounding more and more like a *Marvel* comic). Or I try to ignore it by reminding myself that it's just thoughts, and moving on. But holy crap. The noise.

This is what it's like for me to step into a Starbucks at lunchtime:

Me:	I'm hungry.
Voice:	Are you? You just had breakfast a few hours ago.
Me:	I think I am?
Voice:	Maybe you're thirsty.
Me:	Maybe that's right. I'll get a Frappuccino and have lunch later.
Voice:	A Frappuccino? Why would you choose a beverage that has calories?
Me:	It tastes good.
Voice:	That's not a thing.
Me:	I think it is?
Voice:	It's not.
Me:	It is.
Voice:	If you get a Frappuccino that should be your lunch. Also, make sure it's made with skim milk. And get the small one.

Me: I'm pretty sure I'm hungry. I'll get this sandwich as well.

Voice: If you get a sandwich, you had better get a calorie-free beverage. And not *that* sandwich. That sandwich has too many calories. Put that down. The listed calories are wrong. They're much higher than that. They made a mistake.

Me: I'm going to get a Frappuccino and this sandwich.

Voice: You are weak and disgusting and you are going to get fat and then everyone will see how weak and disgusting you are. Also, make sure you get skim milk!

Me: I got lactose-free.

Voice: Make sure it's not whole milk! That looks too creamy. Those teenage-baristas don't care about using the right milk. Post-millennials are going to make you fat, thirty calories at a time. And that sandwich is huge. Eat half and throw out the rest. No one eats more than half. *No one*. Wait. Is that cheese in there?

Me: Yes. I like cheese.

Voice: If you eat that I will make you feel bad about it for the rest of the day. And tonight, when you're getting undressed I'll point out how fat you are. And then at 4 a.m. when you wake up to pee, I'll remind you of this very moment and keep you up for the rest of the night. I will make you regret the day you ever set foot in this Starbucks [evil cackle].

The cackle was obviously added for dramatic effect (and because I feel like this segment is high on weird and short on jokes). Though a cackle might be a helpful reminder for me that it's not my voice. Because in the moment, it's easy to forget.

Until recently I would have walked out of Starbucks with a black coffee and maybe a plain salad. Now I'm better at ignoring the noise, but it's exhausting, and unrelenting. And like my kids who will nag me until they get what they want and will then find something new to nag about (like magic!), the voice is never satisfied. And the noise never stops.

My friends think I have trouble ordering from a menu simply because I'm indecisive, which I am. But really, it's because the voice is too noisy to let me make a decision. I can't even imagine what it's like not to hear it. Sometimes I play a game—what would I give up to make it stop? A finger (anything but the middle ones)? Hearing in one ear? My sense of smell? The ironic part is that all I have to give up is control.

I've read countless times that there's a weight threshold at which the noise is said to start getting better, a whisper instead of a shout, a whimper instead of a scream. I know I have to get there. If only that voice could shut up long enough for me to do it.

CHAPTER 17

For the past ten months I've been using the services of an online recovery coach (a little like a therapist, but bossier and more opinionated). Her name is Emily; she's really great.

From: Sheri Segal Glick
Subject: Re: Checking in
To: Emily
Date: July 31, 2019, 12:17 p.m.

Hi Emily,

Cottage was good. There was a lot of sitting around, but it was more okay than not. On the first day Elizabeth's (very sweet) husband asked what would happen if I didn't go for a walk by noon. And I had to say that I didn't know, and that I might actually spontaneously combust. The lack of movement felt impossibly hard at times, but overall, it was a lovely couple of days that I know I couldn't have done a few months—or maybe weeks—ago.

Oh and food was also okay. I brought most of the food for the dinners (at my insistence) and lots of snacks (in the form of fruit, sorry) and we both contributed to the lunches. I tried to keep my calorie calculator as muted as possible, but it was still there whirring in the background. Numbers were obviously imprecise, as the bowls and plates (and wine glasses) were new to me. I vividly remember surreptitiously measuring the bowls at the cottage we shared with Kevin and Neil last summer while everyone was still asleep. I was so grateful not to have to do that this time around.

Last night Kirsten and I had plans to conquer two list items—Indian food and movie popcorn. It was meant to be solely a movie-popcorn plan and she added dinner, because she's slammed this week and it was a bit of a now-or-never situation. The dinner was hard. I wasn't at all hungry which set off all the alarm bells (This is excessive! Eating when I'm not hungry will make me fat!) but I ordered a shrimp curry thing in a semi-thick slippery red sauce (that's how it's actually listed on the menu), and it was very good. I didn't eat all of the sauce, or all of the rice, but the shrimp was very shiny and well-coated, and it felt like I had done the challenge in accordance with both the spirit and letter of the law.

The popcorn part was awful. I knew I had to get it, but by the time we arrived at the theater I had a terrible stomachache (maybe nerves, maybe not). Kirsten and I both got our own bags, and she happily ate hers, like a normal person. The theater was not one of the big chains but rather an independent theater, with all the time and money to coat every kernel in yellow coconut oil. It seemed richer and greasier and saltier than Cineplex-popcorn. And in that moment, I couldn't do it. Kirsten kept looking over at me and encouraging me to eat it, but every time I put my hand in the bag, an alarm bell went off in my head, telling me that eating a meal without hunger is one thing, but that following it with a snack without hunger is excessive, and disgusting. I was so conflicted that it was all I could do to not burst into tears. And then the movie ended, and I had eaten no popcorn. I could hardly look Kirsten in the eye. I felt like I'd failed us both. Adding insult to injury, it was raining, and I had to shield the dastardly popcorn from the rain as we crossed the street to get the car (yep, we drove).

When I arrived home, I had a text from Kirsten telling me that I could still do it. And I wrote her back to say that I'd try—I didn't want to be beaten by popcorn, or a crazy voice in my head. And then I sat there staring at it for an hour. Then I brought the popcorn upstairs with me, sat on my bed, and stared it at some more. Finally, around 12:30 a.m., I ate the popcorn. My stomach still hurt, and it felt so scary and awful (triumvirate of fear: eating when I'm not hungry, eating unnecessary calories, eating something when I don't like the taste), but I knew that I couldn't go to bed with the knowledge that Kirsten left work earlier than she needed to so that I wasn't rushed at dinner and so that we would have plenty of time to get movie popcorn.

Sleeping was hard. A child came into my bed somewhere around 3 a.m., and all I could think about was that stupid popcorn (not shockingly, I was—and continue to be—very thirsty). The guilt has been hard to ignore. I did a workout today and walked in 31-degree heat. I know this kind of compensation won't help me. But in the moment, it was the only way to quiet all. that. noise.

Anyway, I'm still glad about the cottage. And the curry. And maybe even the popcorn.

I hope that the transition back to California-life has been smooth.

Sheri

CHAPTER 18

Yesterday at school pickup, I wasn't on my game. I was tired and distracted, so when a friend started talking to me about exercise, my defenses were a little lower than usual. The conversation started innocently enough, with us talking about yoga (which I generally hate but do because I hate meditating even more). Then she asked me if I was still working out at home in the mornings. I could have said yes, but I'm not working out at home in the mornings, so I said no (I didn't want accolades for doing something I've stopped doing, and I've had that conversation enough to know where that was headed).

She asked me why I'd stopped, and I gave a stock answer about boredom or something, by then starting to feel uncomfortable. I should have shut the conversation down right there, with a quick and easy topic change ("I'll be right back, I have to pee!" is my personal favorite, but "There's something in your teeth" and "Is that your kid with his pants down?" also work in a pinch), but I didn't. She suggested nearby gyms I could go to. I told her that I'm not working out at all right now, and she asked why not. Instead of inventing an injury, like a rational person with a working brain would have, I casually said that I am finding cardio kind of addictive and need a break (that's fine, right? People say stuff like that all the time?). My friend—clearly puzzled—said that was a great addiction to have, and that I'm lucky, and why on earth would I stop?

And in keeping with my goal to make things as awkward as humanly possible, I looked at her like she was insane, deflected, and waited patiently for my daughter's next temper tantrum (not to be all braggy, but I can rely on her to have at least three per hour). My kid came through and I've never been happier to be yelled at by a five-year-old.

After the episode I felt awful. I'd accidentally revealed something about myself that was very private, and very weird, and that my friend might think was weird enough to mention to someone else. I also felt awful because part of me agrees with her. An exercise addiction *is* a great thing to have. Why force myself not to do this thing that everyone else wants to do more of? It doesn't even make sense. People *pay* trainers to get them to exercise when they don't feel like it. Left to my own volition, I'll exercise for hours on end. I'm *amazing* at that. I'll prioritize exercise over social engagements, and sleep, and weekends away. I'll not only exercise for hours, but I'll think about exercising for many of the hours that I'm not exercising. I'm really so blessed. I might have missed out on some silly life-stuff, but I have so (!) many workouts under my belt.

Stopping my morning workouts and drastically reducing my walking felt impossible a couple of months ago. The fact that I've been able to do it for the past few weeks makes me feel simultaneously triumphant and like a soft, slothful failure. Not exercising takes up more energy than exercising because it's on my mind constantly. Not only do I miss the act of working out, I miss not feeling lazy, and guilty, and conflicted, and scared all the time.

Sometimes I flirt with the idea that I can do a moderate amount of exercise. I tell myself that I can do forty minutes of cardio a few days a week and that it will be enough, but that's probably not true. It will probably inch back up, and before I know it, I won't be able to go away for a weekend or accept a drive home in the rain. I also flirt with the idea that all of that wouldn't be so bad in exchange for thinness and less noise. Recovery is total bullshit. I'm never not on the precipice of giving up.

But I'm pretty sure that I'd like to know what it feels like to rest without guilt. I didn't let myself do that after childbirth, or while I was in labor (you haven't experienced a contraction unless you've had one while using the elliptical machine). I exercised the day of my sweet grandmother's funeral, almost missed the LSAT because I was out running, and worked out every day of every vacation I've ever taken.

An exercise addiction is not a great thing to have. Balance is a great thing to have, and the only way to get there is by being here—this place where I don't get to do what I want, so I can find out what it's like to want something independently of my eating disorder.

Though I still wish that I could go for a run right now. Or at least a really, really fast walk. Maybe even a yoga class.

CHAPTER 19

To whom it may concern,

You are receiving this email quiz because you are someone who has said boneheaded things to me about my body/your body/ other people's bodies/my diet/your diet/my exercise habits/your exercise habits on more than one occasion, despite knowing about my recovery from a restrictive eating disorder and exercise addiction.

If you recognize some of the things you've said, don't feel bad, everyone says boneheaded things sometimes. Maybe this quiz will help you say them less.

1. **When I tell you that I am not exercising right now, the appropriate response is to:**

    (a) tell me that it must be really hard and that you could never do that because you like eating too much

    (b) tell me that I should find some friends who live in the suburbs who don't care about exercise and who are already overweight

    (c) say over and over that you don't understand and ask repeatedly why I can't do a little bit

(d)   invite me to go running with you

(e)   say that you know that it's hard for me and you are around
if I need a distraction

2.   **When I tell you that I burst a pair of pants at the seams
yesterday, the appropriate response is to:**

(a)   mostly ignore it

(b)   tell me that they are crappy quality and you ripped yours
too

(c)   laugh

(d)   tell me that you will let me know if I start getting "really,
really fat"

(e)   anything but (d)

3.   **You went for the most amazing long run today, do you:**

(a)   tell me all about how great it was and how much you wish
I could have come

(b)   not tell me about it unless I ask you where you were

(c)   not tell me about it directly, but then tell me that you don't
know why you can't talk to me about exercise and how
much you hate keeping secrets from me

(d)   post a photo of yourself in your running gear and tag me

4.   **We are at a social gathering (with food). Do you:**

(a)   talk about how much weight you've lost since going carb-
free

(b)   talk about how bad sugar is for people and how addictive
it is

(c)   point at things and ask me how many calories are in them

(d)   talk about how you can have cake because you are going to "work it off" tomorrow at spin class

(e)   none of the above

5. **I tell you that I am having a really hard time right now and that I want to quit recovery. Do you:**

(a)   tell me to turn my frown upside down/choose joy/don't worry be happy

(b)   remind me of all the reasons to keep going or ask if I want to talk about it

(c)   tell me that I look great and healthy and stopping here would be fine

(d)   ask me if that means we can start running again

6. **I tell you that I ate fries today for the first time since childhood. Do you:**

(a)   say that's a great way to put on weight if I'm still trying to gain some

(b)   congratulate me on my achievement

(c)   say that you love fries and will have them with me next time

(d)   tell me that you love fries but that you don't eat them because they are too fattening

7. **I tell you that I am trying to recover from an eating disorder. Do you:**

(a)   tell me that you always knew something was up and that you are glad I'm getting help

(b)   tell me that you always knew something was up and then ask me about what you should do to lose weight since I clearly know all the tricks

(c)   tell me that everyone's eating is disordered, and that it's no biggie and I'm fine

(d)   tell me that you've always wished for an eating disorder, but just for a few weeks so you could lose those last ten pounds

Answer key: e, e, b, e, b, b/c, a

CHAPTER 20

I mentioned the famous muffins at the children's hospital to a friend (in the context of getting one for her son, who had to go for an X-ray, not because I wanted to meet there for breakfast). My kids are crazy for those muffins. It's their big treat after a gastroenterology appointment or a few stitches. It struck me in the moment that regardless of whether the hospital muffins are truly excellent, it's weird that we all love them. Or at least the reason is weird. When I used to stay in the hospital, it was one of the few foods I wasn't afraid of—I would have as many as three a day. What was a comfort food to me as an anorexic teenager has become a family favorite.

And this got me wondering what other weird things from my so-called invisible eating disorder have spilled onto my kids. They are all very good walkers (because I never want to drive), and they've grown up watching me work out in our home gym, so they seem to like exercise. They love nutritious vegetables, like broccoli, cucumbers, and squash, because they know I do (and presumably not because these are foods that are also filling and low-calorie). But they also all really love gum, as though it's a delicious minty adult delicacy rather than something I used to pop into my mouth multiple times a day to stop myself from eating.

I don't talk about bodies except in the context of what they can do and how many shapes and sizes they come in. Though I wonder what else they notice. Do they think that in order for the scale to work one has to get off and on three times? Or do they think that mommies only eat one kind of cereal for breakfast and never use sauces or dressings? Does it matter that we often don't eat the same foods? Did it count for something the other week when my daughter and I shared a cookie? Does she need to see me eating more cookies?

I often feel like recovery is stealing time from my children. I'm preoccupied. I have homework. And I'm often scared and conflicted. I frequently long for the days where my food choices came without recovery-value judgments (plain tofu and broccoli again? Great!) and I could work out my anxiety with some cardio. I don't know what my kids notice, but they certainly notice when I'm in a bad mood, even if they don't know that it's because my pants feel too tight, and I'm not allowed to exercise.

I have never uttered the word "diet" or "calorie" in front of my children. I tell them every day that the way they look is infinitely less important than who they are. But what happens if they figure out I believe that for everyone other than myself? That I place so much of my personal worth on my appearance, just like my mom does on hers (and mine).

On days recovery feels hard and pointless, I can almost convince myself that my kids are oblivious, and that my behavior has no impact on them (or that my other parenting mistakes are so egregious, that food is the last thing we should worry about) but how can I model healthy eating habits without really understanding what those are?

There have been some amazing developments lately in eating disorder research. Scientists keep learning more about the genetic component of eating disorders. This doesn't mean that if you have the genetics you are destined to develop one. Though it's pretty ridiculous for me to try to convince myself that if one of them does end up with an eating disorder, and I haven't fixed mine, that it won't somehow be my fault.

CHAPTER 21

About six months ago, I slipped and fell down my basement stairs. I hit my head so hard that I saw stars like they do in old cartoons, and then flashes, and then weird zigzags. I also suspected I had fractured my tailbone. My husband was away, and my kids were sleeping upstairs, so I shut one eye, held my phone about an inch from my face, and Googled "concussions" and then "death from concussion." I decided (in my internet-confirmed concussed state) that the chances of dying in my sleep were too low to warrant bothering any friends after 11 p.m., so I took two Advil and went to bed, making sure to tidy my bathroom a bit in case I did indeed die in my sleep. *At least* five of my closest friends live within four blocks of my house, but I chose to risk the (albeit small) possibility of my children finding me dead over waking any of them up.

There are few things I find more meaningful, and often joyful, than helping the people I care about. And there are few things I find harder than asking those same people for help. I have trouble believing that I am anything less than an incompetent burden when I have to rely on my friends. Realizing I need help and then asking for that help has been one of the hardest things about recovery (except for the eating and no-exercise parts).

It's hard because I don't know what I need sometimes. It's hard because even when I do know what I need, I don't necessarily want it. It's hard because I have to explain what I can't do, and why I can't do that thing, and I'm forced to acknowledge that none of it makes any sense. It's hard because I feel weird and needy and crazy. It's hard because sometimes anorexia twists things and innocent comments wound me.

It's hard because I know that I'm asking for so much more than for someone to drag themselves out of their warm bed to go watch my kids while I go get my concussion treated.

I sometimes imagine what it would be like to have a friend like me who asks to go out for dinner. Presumably (?) I say yes, and we choose a restaurant, and we go. Initially things are as expected: the server comes and fills our water, and we chat, and we get wine. And then the server brings the dinner menus and my friend starts staring at it with an intensity that's usually reserved for parking tickets in her husband's name. The server comes back and sees my friend still carefully reading the menu and asks if she needs the large-print copy. He comes back again. And again. And finally, he asks if we're ready to order. I look over at my friend who is now on the verge of tears, and maybe I make a joke about how I'll never be able to return to that particular restaurant. I'm not completely joking. Especially because my friend still. can't. fucking. order. And then eventually she orders, and then she doesn't stop talking about whether she should change her order. And then the food comes, and my friend stares at it, and maybe she cries. And I wonder if a very public breakup with my friend would endear me to the staff, who now have questions about both of us.

But it's not over. I have to sit there uncomfortably while my friend eats whatever has been placed in front of her. And it takes ages. And my friend is truly terrible company because she is so distracted by the pasta-curry-stirfry-salad-bowl-French-fries-pizza.

Sounds amazing, right?

Now imagine that you're the friend. How quick would you be to ask someone to come eat with you? What if you knew that the only way to learn to eat the hard things is by eating them, but that sometimes you can't do it yourself because you need someone to talk over the noise. Would you ask?

It's important to me to make people—especially people I care about—feel valued and appreciated. And this feels like the exact opposite of that. Sometimes I disregard advice. I ask the same questions over and over (and sometimes ignore the answers that are given). I frustrate the people I most want to make happy.

Sometimes that frustration is palpable. And I'm ashamed that I'm so much work. And that I'm so not fun when it comes to things that are easy and fun for most people.

Sometimes I feel like I'm sucking the air out of the room and out of the friendship. And that I'm ruining everything.

And other times, I can find the words and the courage to say, "I know we've already talked about this so many times, but the noise in my head is so loud right now, I can't access what we said. I need you to talk over the noise and to say it all again."

Or "please talk me out of giving up."

Or "please come have an awful, terrible, horrible, awkward meal with me."

And my friends step up. And I'm indescribably grateful. And it changes my life a tiny bit, or a lot.

CHAPTER 22

Emily has convinced me to stop doing workouts on my elliptical machine. She had me write up a list of the scariest foods I could imagine and then cast a spell whereby I was able to eat my way through that entire list. Because of her I have been able to endure consecutive days of almost no movement, order food off a menu, slice cheese without a food scale, and eat it on buttered toast. She said I should be open about the illness with more of my friends, and I listened to her, and it was okay—better than okay actually, because now I don't have to wear a mask quite as often.

And yet when we designed a test to see whether I needed the structure of a day hospital program, I failed. And this failure is just one more to add to a tome of failures. This coach is insightful and creative and more intelligent than most people. And she understands my illness in a way that I don't. And I still keep coming back to her with failure after failure.

So now I need to decide whether to do a day-hospital program. It's twelve weeks, five days a week, nine hours per day (except Fridays, where it's only five or six). I will be forced to eat meals served on trays, waxen casseroles and euphemized "chef's specials" that come with two-percent milk and watery side salads glimmering with fluorescent orange dressing, stale little rolls with pats of margarine wrapped in foil, and anemic bowls of canned fruit. I won't be allowed to exercise. I will spend hours a day talking about feelings with seven other women, at least some of whom will be younger-thinner-sicker-simpler than me. Every day I will have to walk into the hospital adjacent to the children's hospital, where I spent so many days, weeks, months of my childhood trapped, where my tears made up part of the water system, by way of tear-soaked sheets and prolonged showers. This sister adult hospital smells exactly the same as the children's did thirty years ago, as though the air has been kept safely in a time capsule (or, a windowless hospital) and flows freely through the two long hallways that join them together.

The dietician already hates me. She has me cast as the Danny Zuko of the group. She remembers me from the Readiness Program I had to participate in to stay on the list for the day-hospital. Spoiler: I wasn't ready. She also read in my file that I was non-compliant in the psycho educational group that I did *in 1990* and swears she remembers me. True to (rebellious) form, I argue and tell her that the statute of limitations for summary conviction offenses in Canada is six months. Therefore, holding me accountable nearly *thirty years* after I was forced to do the program by my parents as a condition of stopping weigh-ins at the Children's, feels a little rich. She disagrees. She says I'm too smart and that I use my intelligence to argue. I resist the urge to tell her I'm not that smart but that she's a dumdum, which is why I seem smart by comparison. Instead, I explain I'm not trying to argue, but that I have a lot of questions. I'm terrified, and I'm not sure she believes me.

She peppers me with questions: "What's changed? Why now? What do you expect? Do you know that you can't exercise? That we won't stop you from gaining even after you pass your target? Did you know you have been ill for a very, very long time?"

The feeling of being a rebellious teenager forced into treatment is imprinted on my soul. It rushes to the surface like a helium balloon, and I have to keep pushing it back down, reminding myself that I'm here voluntarily. I have so much anger at that hospital for their cruelty and their lack of understanding. For all those wasted years. I don't know if I can go back.

And also, I'm pretty sure I hate that dietician and her socks and sandals.

The hospital might be my last best hope. The forced confinement might finally end my compulsion to exercise. The gawdawful meal plan might get me out of the caloric deficit that in clearer moments I believe exists. The weight gain (oh my god, the weight gain) might be the thing that finally turns the volume down on the incessant, relentless voice of my eating disorder.

I will be giving up control, and time with my children, and time with my friends and time volunteering at the school. I will be giving up the freedom to go out for lunch, or to go shopping on a whim, or to sit down and write when the mood strikes. I worry that people will forget about me, or replace me, or find out why I'm not around. I will have to make up excuses for the people in my life, including my kids. I will be forced to admit that I couldn't do this without an extra level of care. That I failed.

And there is no promise that any of it will work. I might give up my freedom, and time, and control, and moments with my children, for nothing. That might be a greater disappointment than I am prepared to handle.

I tell the dietician I've been using the services of an eating disorder recovery coach. "An athletic coach?" she asks for what seems like the one hundredth time. "No, the *opposite* of that," I say, exasperated.

I would like nothing more than to carry on with coaching—to skip the meal plan, and the confinement, and the awful, tedious group therapy. But maybe it's exactly what I need. Some of my ambivalence about the program is not mine but my eating disorder's. This program poses an existential threat to its existence.

My eating disorder whispers to me that it's keeping me safe. It moans that everyone else is lying to me, that there is nothing more important than taking up as little space as possible in the world. It shouts that no one will respect me if my body doesn't look a certain way, that I'm fine and normal and my coach, and dearest friends, and the people at the hospital are wrong and will ruin me. It shrieks that it knows best. It howls that I am worthless without it.

And it's so hard for me not to listen. It's sometimes impossible for me to tease my thoughts apart from those of this demon that's been taking up real estate in my brain since I was twelve years old.

CHAPTER 23

Day Hospital Program: Day 1

9:06 a.m. Get off the elevator. Try to act like casual visitor as a way of dealing with embarrassment of getting off in front of a giant sign reading MENTAL HEALTH.

9:07 a.m. Check in seven minutes late because my kids aren't used to the new morning routine and because I didn't account for morning traffic.

9:08 a.m. I'm sent to the waiting room. I concentrate on not getting coughed on by the heavy breather next to me and not being spotted by my neighbor, who works in the department. Wish I had a paper bag to put over my head, which would solve both problems.

9:39 a.m. Someone finally comes to collect me. I silently bid adieu to the heavy breather.

9:42 a.m. Meet with the social worker who asks me some questions and gives me some papers to put in the three-ring binder I was told to bring. None of the papers have holes.

10:08 a.m. Meet with the nurse practitioner who asks me all the same questions the social worker just asked. She's kind to me. I start to cry.

10: 20 a.m. Meet with the IT guy (actually a grad student in charge of putting all patient survey data into the system). He explains how the surveys work. I focus on not crying. It goes medium.

10:24 a.m. Meet with the dietician and another nurse. They take my blood pressure, height, and weight. Thrilled to see I haven't shrunk. Am anxious about the weight as I'm wearing jeans and a heavy sweater, and I nervously drank a ton of water in the waiting room. Make a mental note to recreate the exact same conditions for next Tuesday's weigh-in.

10:35 a.m. Am directed to the set of rooms where the day program takes place. I walk into a large empty room, its white walls decorated with inspirational posters, hefty neutral-colored chairs, plastic stools, and a wall of white boards. I open the door that leads to the adjoining kitchen where I find the other seven patients sitting at a long narrow table.

10:36 a.m. Meet the other women in the program. Sort of. We don't exchange names. They are all doing their own thing (coloring, homework, talking). One of them tells me that Tuesdays are homework catch-up days, and since I am new and therefore have no homework, I'm free until noon. I restlessly sit at the table and focus on not-crying.

10:46 a.m. I follow some smokers out of the building, text my friends to let them know I'm still alive, and go for a walk.

12:00 p.m. Lunch is served. Sweet Jesus.

12:14 p.m. Busy-body patient points out I haven't finished all my margarine. I'm forced to spread the rest on the bite of roll that remains.

12:21 p.m. I am reprimanded by the psychologist supervising the meal for not drinking the juice at the bottom of my canned fruit cocktail.

12:22 p.m. I try to determine if she is joking.

12:23 p.m. She is not. I drink the juice.

12:30 p.m. Fill out my food journal. I circle SCARED SAD ANXIOUS ANGRY as my predominant feelings.

12:45 p.m. I'm sent for bloodwork. The tech ties a rubber band around my arm so tightly that I immediately lose feeling in my fingers and ignores me when I tell her the band is too tight. There is blood everywhere. I look her in the eye, tell her she is terrible at her job, and go outside for another walk. My arm is still bleeding.

2:45 p.m. Snack. My stomach is still churning from lunch. I see that two of the other patients aren't having a snack. I ask if I can have mine later as well. The dietician says no so forcefully that I wonder if she has misunderstood my question and thinks maybe I said, "can I pack an alligator?" rather than "can I have my snack later?"

3:00 p.m. I'm in trouble. I haven't been able to eat my snack. I'm permitted to bring it into the group room as a one-time-super-special exception.

4:30 p.m. Group ends. Still holding my fucking snack. Dietician uses a combination of threats and coercion to get me to eat it. I feel like I'm going to be ill, but also, I'm grateful to her.

5:00 p.m. Dinner is served. I burst into tears. Busy-body patient reminds me to finish all my salad dressing and margarine. Empty containers are examined with the same intensity as a *Bachelorette* contestant examining her diamond engagement ring.

5:20 p.m. I ask what my main course was supposed to be for the purposes of my food log. The patient across from me laughs. I decide that I like her. The psychologist supervising the meal admonishes me, and then tells me what it was (zucchini casserole). I decide that I like her even less than I like zucchini casserole.

5:30 p.m. Fill out my food journal. I circle SCARED SAD ANXIOUS ANGRY as my predominant feelings.

5:35 p.m. We go around the table and talk about how we felt during the meal. I don't mention how much my stomach hurts. Or how scary-demoralizing-sad that was. I do learn that I'm allowed to say my dinner wasn't to my taste, but not that it was an insult to both zucchini and casseroles.

6:00 p.m. Freedom.

Day 2

8:40 a.m. Only two thirds of my kids are ready for school. I leave my oldest at home and tell him he has to be at school before the bell.

8:45 a.m. Youngest child has a meltdown when I ask her sister to walk her into the schoolyard. Spend more time convincing her to go with her sister than it would have taken me to walk her myself.

8:52 a.m. Traffic.

8:59 a.m. Anxiously drive into a cement barrier in the parking lot. Break many parts of my car including one piece I didn't even know was breakable.

9:04: a.m. Get off the elevator. Try to act like a confused visitor as a way of dealing with embarrassment of getting off in front of a giant sign reading MENTAL HEALTH.

9:06 a.m. Arrive to DBT group late. The door is locked. Everyone watches me take my seat. I'm told it's the wrong seat. Everyone watches me move seats.

9:40 a.m. Receive text from school office administrator. Oldest child hasn't arrived. Try to reach my house cleaner.

9:45 a.m. Leave the room to call my oldest child. Tell him he has to go to school. Call school and say he's on his way.

10:20 a.m. Get another text from the school. Son hasn't arrived.

10:25 a.m. Break. Call home again.

10:30 a.m. Another group. I'm hungry but have been told I can't switch my afternoon snack for a morning one.

11:00 a.m. Get text that oldest child is still not at school

11:30 a.m. Break. Go for a walk while furiously trying to locate oldest child.

11:50 a.m. Receive notice that son has just arrived at school

12:00 p.m. Lunch is served. *Fuckity fuck.* I ask the nurse practitioner supervising to make sure the meal on my tray wasn't a mistake. It apparently wasn't. I contemplate walking—no sprinting—out of the room.

12:03 p.m. Busy-body patient at the other end of the table loudly informs me that while my food journal should be in the room, people don't traditionally bring their whole binder in. I ask if she is worried about germs or if it will affect the enjoyment of her lunch. She says no. I leave the binder in the room.

12:05 p.m. Notice again how hard it is to breathe, chew, and hold back tears simultaneously.

12:30 p.m. Fill out my food journal. I circle SCARED SAD ANXIOUS ANGRY as my predominant feelings.

1:00 p.m. Another group.

2:30 p.m. We collectively go downstairs for a snack. A patient tells me I'm not allowed to walk down the down escalator because it's a "behavior." She informs me that we also aren't allowed to use the stairs. I make a mental note to find the stairs.

2:45 p.m. I am able to eat my snack without incident despite still being uncomfortably full from lunch.

3:00 p.m. More group.

4:30 p.m. Break. I find the stairs and go outside for a walk.

4:55 p.m. Arrive back for dinner. Am told that dinner is delayed by half an hour and that we won't be allowed to leave until 6:30, rather than 6. I call my sitter and ask her to make the kids eggs for dinner as I won't be home on time to feed them. My youngest cries when she hears that I'm going to be late.

5:10 p.m. I go for a walk around the hospital. Bump into the social worker on my way back to the stairs. Pretend I'm lost. Am thankful for all my improv training.

5:30 p.m. Dinner is served. *Fuckity fuck fuck.*

5:31 p.m. I follow another patient to the microwave to melt my cheese into my chilli at her suggestion. I'm informed that no one is allowed to microwave anything more than thirty seconds. I've already broken up the cheese and put it into the chilli. There's no going back.

5:35 p.m. I eat chilli with half-melted warmish chunks of cheese in it.

5:45 p.m. A patient notices a grape that she's put into her mouth is rotten. She is told to eat it anyway. I laugh out loud at the absurdity. She swallows the grape.

5:50 p.m. Fill out my food journal. I circle SCARED SAD ANXIOUS ANGRY as my predominant feelings.

6:30 p.m. Freedom

Day 3

8:45 a.m. Youngest child has a meltdown at school drop-off. She won't let her sister walk her into the yard. I lose it and yell that I can't be late again. An acquaintance overhears and says she'll keep an eye on her. I'm mortified and so grateful I could cry.

9:01 a.m. Get off the elevator. Try to act like I work there as a way of dealing with embarrassment of getting off in front of a giant sign reading MENTAL HEALTH.

9:03 a.m. Arrive to DBT group late. The door is locked. Everyone watches me take my seat.

9:15 a.m. Listen to another patient talk about her life, and how she feels about herself. I cry, but not for myself this time.

10:20 a.m. Realize that I'm really hungry. Regret not having finished my breakfast.

10:30 a.m. Relationship group. A patient reports that her husband has said that he can't listen to her talk about how hard recovery is anymore, that he's sick and tired of all of it. My stomach churns as I think about the burden I have become, and how much I've been relying on my closest friends. I wonder how many feel the same way.

11:43 a.m. Break. Check texts. Kirsten has written that her day has been a productive one so far. I resolve to stop bugging her about my stupid recovery shit while she is at work.

11:45 a.m. Go for a micro walk. Contemplate not going back in.

12:05 p.m. Lunch is served. *Fuckity fuck fuck fuck.* It's too scary. I don't think I can do it. My stomach growls.

12:06 p.m. I notice the dietician is distracted while I'm pouring my salad dressing. I leave a miniscule amount in the container and throw out the packaging with the rest of my garbage.

12:08 p.m. Dietician asks to see my garbage. I tell her I've already thrown it out. She tells me to go get it. My head starts buzzing. I can't decide whether I have time to pour out the tiny bit of remaining dressing while I'm digging through the garbage. I fatefully decide that I don't.

12:08 p.m. She scolds me like I am a child who has been caught stealing and tells me that I have to use it. I tell her that I'm not using garbage-dressing.

12:09 p.m. She stares me down.

12:09 p.m. I stare back.

12:10 p.m. I ask if I can use a new dressing, but only the amount I have remaining. She agrees.

12:11 p.m. I commence the complicated task of leaving the exact right amount in the new container of dressing. Dietician grows impatient and tells me I have to use what's left. I argue that it's too much. She tells me it's my punishment for being sneaky earlier.

12:12 p.m. Another stare down.

12:12 p.m. She tells me that I have ten seconds to decide whether to use the dressing or leave. I am aware that we are making a scene. I'm mortified. It's a boulder rolling down a hill. Also, I don't want to eat the extra dressing.

12:13 p.m. She tells me that my time is up and asks what I am going to do. I look at the rest of that meal and imagine myself trying to eat it, and how guilty-bloated-panicked I'll feel afterward. I look at the salad dressing. The dietician says again that I have to leave if I'm not eating, and that if I leave, I can't come back.

12:14 p.m. I storm out over half a teaspoon of dirty salad dressing. The remorse and shame and sadness and regret won't fully hit me for about forty-eight hours. I won't be able to shake that off.

CHAPTER 24

Walking out of the hospital is a relief. I'm relieved that I can eat (or not eat!) whatever I want for lunch. I'm relieved that I can pick up my kids from school. I'm relieved that I can go to yoga with my friends the next day and help distribute pizza at the school on pizza day. I'm relieved that I'm not going to get fat (at least not immediately on a diet of zucchini casseroles and two-percent milk).

I text four close friends on the way out or just after I've left. I text my husband once I'm home. I don't text Kirsten. I don't want to send her a text in the middle of her busy day because I know that she'll be upset that I've left and I don't want my recovery drama to bleed into what sounded like a pretty good workday for her. But really, there's no one that I want to talk to more.

The first thing I do after eating my not-scary-chosen-entirely-by-me lunch is to draft her an email that I plan to send at the end of her workday (she lives in another city). As the hours go by, I have a sinking feeling that my email is going to be as well-received as a series of Tweets from stable genius Donald Trump.

I leave the email in my drafts folder, put the kids to bed, and meet my friend Elizabeth for wine. I'm able to make light of the entire episode. We laugh over fruit cocktail juice as a beverage and garbage-dressing, but even in the moment it feels like a performance—one of those under-rehearsed routines about eating disorder treatment that have become so ridiculously commonplace in the stand-up comedy circuit.

I'd planned to send the email to Kirsten on my walk home, but I still can't bring myself to do it. Finally, I send it when I arrive home, sitting on the stairs, coat and boots still on. It's past her usual bedtime, and I don't think I'll hear back. But I do. She's not upset, she's livid. She is so angry that she says she can't write anymore and that she'll be in touch after she cools down. That email dashes any keeping-my-small-pants elation I'm still hanging onto.

The next day is Friday, and it feels almost like the day hospital program was all a bad dream. I get to walk my kids to school, and chat with people in the schoolyard, and go to yoga and bake muffins for after school snack. I even do a workout (because who am I answering to? no one!). Though every so often, I find myself thinking about the day program and what they're up to. Riding on the escalator? Eating half-melted cheese? Actually talking about meaningful things that will make their lives better? The remorse starts to seep in, like rain through a cracked window, as my relief mutates into a sense of painful, sinking, confusing loss. It doesn't make any sense. All I had wanted was not to be at the program. And now I'm not at the program, and I'm still not happy. Maybe I do need to be inside a unit with a big sign reading MENTAL HEALTH, as it's becoming pretty apparent to me that I don't have mine.

Saturday morning, I hear from Kirsten. She is so hurt, which is the part of the entire episode that makes me the saddest and still brings tears to my eyes every time I think about it. I had expected upset and disappointment, but not anger, and certainly not hurt. She's hurt that I hadn't called to tell her I was leaving. She feels like I owed her at least that much, because I did. She spent countless hours talking to me about whether to do the program and persuading me that it was the right choice. She encouraged me and supported me and read my pro/con lists and sat with me while I cried. And she was the very last person I told that I quit. I'm not sure that she believes me when I tell her I was trying to give her a break from me and my stupid problems. She knows that she is the one person who might have convinced me to stay, and now I know that too. I don't know what to do with her pain, or mine. Or her anger (at me) and mine (at me). So, I walk and walk and walk. And I cry.

We talk the next day. She says she isn't angry anymore. I have a much harder time letting go of my anger with myself.

On Monday I call one of the directors of the day hospital program to see if I can have my spot back. She says that it's too late, but that maybe they'll take me back in a couple of months. I email Emily, who says I'll need to come up with a very different recovery plan if I'm going to resume with her. There's no point resuming coaching if I'm unwilling to change the habits we both know are keeping me tethered to my eating disorder.

I feel only adrenaline (and guilt and shame and remorse) running through my veins. The urge to restrict is unremitting. It seems like the only thing that can make the rest of it feel better. Strangely though, despite the not-insignificant caloric deficit, my weight stays almost the same. It doesn't make any sense, it's scary and frustrating (if I don't know how to lose weight, and I don't how to recover, and I don't know how to not-hurt my friends, what the actual fuck do I know?)

I realize I'll have to restrict even more if I want to attain the high that I'm chasing. It seems like a reasonable price to pay, given how sad (and fat) I feel. It seems like the best DIY-feel-good-makeover project that I can come up with. Except every once in a while, it feels wrong and dark and like I am on the precipice of a cliff. These tiny moments of clarity are still the only thing keeping me from falling over into a very deep hole (can someone fall off a cliff into a hole? Yes?).

My friends notice. They see that I'm drinking less wine and making excuses around meals. One night Elizabeth and I take our kids to the movies and dinner and I send my (wrongly) dressed salad back, and she expresses her disappointment so loudly ("You're *still doing this? Maybe you should be back at that program.*") that my embarrassment seeps into the next day, and the one after that. My kids and I stay for an impromptu dinner at the home of two of my best friends, Kevin and Neil, and I'm unable to eat, afraid of all the food (which feels like the epitome of hypocrisy while I'm lecturing my fussy five-year-old about trying all the things). Kevin and Neil are among the safest people for me to talk to—they know about all of it. I don't say anything. I push the food around on my plate and finally exhale when we start bringing the dishes into the kitchen.

That week, the subject of Neil's forty-fifth birthday comes up and all he wants is to go out to a fancy vegan restaurant (ignore the oxymoron) for an eight-course tasting menu with me and Kevin. He rarely asks for anything so I agree to go, with the terrifying knowledge that I can't just not eat anything as that will make his birthday about me. The lead-up is horror-movie (or teased-bangs-and-blue-eye-shadow) scary, but it's an exceptionally lovely night, because it means so much to him. I end that night with the understanding that being able to participate in that dinner is so much more meaningful than the size of my pants, and that I don't want to be someone who sends salads back, or who counts wine calories, or who misses (or almost misses) her best friends' birthday dinners.

And then, like a wave, all the feelings come back. The guilt and shame and sense of failure. I have a very hard time with one of my kids, and all I want to do is walk and not-eat. I want to numb the guilt about failing at the program, and failing at parenting, and all the wasted years. I want confirmation that even though I can't control anything else, I can still control my body. And when I weigh myself and my weight is down a bit, I am so relieved. But holy fuck that's so fucking stupid. I'm making it worse.

I can't rely on fleeting moments of happiness over a lost pound or two to make it better. If I want a full life I'm going to have to live with the discomfort of tight pants and a shrinking thigh gap until they stop mattering. A few pounds aren't worth everything I'm giving up; they aren't worth the rest of my life. But it's so noisy inside my head. It feels like an actual war. Right now, every meal and snack and moment of stillness comes with a battle wound.

My husband says that this is the part of the book where I figure out how to do it on my own and get better. I'm not sure if I should be playing the *Rocky* theme song for this part (or maybe a less-exercisey motivational theme song?). Today I'm doing my best just to stay out of the very warm, inviting hole.

CHAPTER 25

I almost died when I was in the eleventh grade. And not in the fun and carefree way you hear about people almost dying in the eleventh grade.

I'd begged my parents to let me audition for the local arts high school at the end of grade eight, and they had said no, worrying I might meet kids who smoked or whose parents were divorced (they very much looked up to superdad Bill Cosby). Then for whatever reason, my parents agreed to let me audition in the spring of grade ten (see kids? Two years of persistent nagging is all it takes!) and I was accepted into the drama and vocal music programs, and I chose drama. I had been hospitalized twice that year, so while I was sad to leave my friends at my old school, I was excited to start at a new school where no one knew about any of it.

Early that summer I bumped into a guy I'd acted with previously, and it turned out he went to the arts school. He invited me to a series of parties, and I hung out with my new classmates over the next couple of months. I met some nice kids (who actually did smoke! Happily I'd had all of that practice at the hospital) and by the time school started in September, I was securely part of my new school's social scene. Classes were fun. I had fun new friends. Boys liked me. I got to play Lysistrata in our fall play. Frosty lipstick was in. Everyone wore a lot of black and acted like they were on the TV show *Fame*. Life was grand. And then I stopped getting hungry.

I don't think what happened next could be considered a relapse because I was never better. It's crazy to imagine now, but I had never once heard the term "recovery." But I hadn't been completely not-eating, and I was happy with the way I looked (while wearing a heavily padded bra). Then I lost my appetite, and with that, the ability to eat. Unlike when the same thing happened when I was an adult, it didn't occur to me that I should force myself, that I needed to take in some calories, somehow. I just told myself that when I got hungry, I'd eat. It was years before the term "intuitive eating" would be coined, but that's what I thought I was doing—listening to my body. And my body wasn't hungry.

I can now see that I was actually starving and that my body had decided to stop sending hunger signals to save energy, just like it didn't bother wasting energy on body heat or on menstrual periods, but that was not something that had ever been explained to me. The psychiatrist at the children's hospital later described it as "hunger denial crossover syndrome," but that's bullshit. My body was simply too weak to get hungry.

Occasionally, I did get hungry very late at night, but I didn't feel like I could eat anything high calorie (read: that contained calories) at that hour because if Richard-Simmons-Suzanne-Sommers-Jane-Fonda had taught me anything, it was that the only thing worse than eating when you aren't hungry is eating in the middle of the night. Sure, starving yourself is worse than both of those things, but they didn't touch on that. So instead, I would eat lettuce and vinegar or some carrot sticks and go back to bed, promising myself I'd eat a proper breakfast if I woke up hungry. And of course, I never did. I think that on some level I knew I was making life-destroying mistake after life-destroying mistake, but the eating disorder drowned all that out.

By late fall, my weight had fallen to a number I still can't wrap my head around or say out loud. I've maybe told one other person that crazy number, but I don't want to ask her. That number is confirmation that no matter how filmy my memories are of that time, I was really, really ill, and there was no way people didn't notice. There was no good reason I should have lived.

And yet, I still couldn't eat. I started wearing my winter jacket all the time, even to class. My new classmates knew there was something wrong but didn't know me well enough to bring it up. My parents knew there was something wrong, but didn't know how thin I was because I always dressed in layers, and it wasn't obvious in my face (I remember my mother being in the room while I was changing my pants about a month after I was hospitalized and audibly gasping upon seeing my legs in thick black tights).

The thing I remember the most from that time was the cold. It's not like the cold from being outside in the winter, or when the air conditioning at a movie theater in summer is too strong, and you've naively shown up in shorts and a T-shirt, as opposed to a parka. It was constant and painful, and I felt it in my bones. I would drink scalding mugs of tea, right out of the microwave, which gave me blisters in my throat and on my soft palate. I would take searing-hot baths that would turn my skin bright pink. I'd stay in the water until I was sweating, only for the cold to return seconds after I got out. My stomach hurt much of the time (a diet of iceberg lettuce, white vinegar, and diet coke might sound classy, but it's hell on your digestion), and I would beat myself up for days for having eaten an apple that I hadn't *truly* needed (because no hunger), but it's the biting cold I can still almost feel.

One day around late November, I was standing in front of the full-length mirror in the school bathroom, and two girls in my class told me that if I didn't eat something, I was going to drop dead. It was the first time I realized that my anorexia wasn't a secret. I shrugged and awkwardly left the bathroom (I've never been great with compliments). I still know both of them and can say with certainty they were not being malicious or making fun of me. They were kind girls—now kind women—who were freaked out and didn't know what else to say. They probably felt like maybe that would get through to me, but by then I was so numb I don't think I would have flinched if they had pulled out a knife and threatened to kill me if I didn't eat something.

I was hospitalized later that week. My dad picked me up from school and we drove to a strange office tower that appeared to be closed. The doctor was waiting for us and let us in. She weighed me, took my blood pressure, listened to my heart, and sent me directly to the hospital. She met us in Emergency, and I was admitted immediately.

I don't have much to say about that time. It was miserable, and the same. The teachers at the hospital school were sad to see me and horrified by how thin I had become. One cried. My friends at the hospital were glad to see me. The nurses were annoyed, as usual (most of the nurses didn't like us. They saw us as manipulative pains in the butt, who took them away from kids who didn't choose to be ill). I hated my new, stricter doctor, but she probably saved my life.

I just wish that rather than threatening me with tube feeding every time the voice in my head wouldn't let me eat, and wheeling my bed into the hallway every time I was on bed rest, someone had explained to me that this didn't have to be my life. That anorexia wasn't my destiny. That I was ruining my bones and wasting my childhood (because really, I was still a child). I wish that someone had explained that I hadn't been ill for that long—five years is a drop in the bucket compared to a lifetime—and that I could learn to be well. I wish one person had told me that what my body looked like was not the most important thing about me. I wish that the medical team had been kind, or less menacing.

I left the hospital after about fourteen weeks. I was still underweight, but no longer dangerously medically unstable. I vowed never to go back. And aside from a quick three-week mini vacation there a couple of months later, and that gawdawful psycho-educational group at the adult hospital that I would agree to do to get my parents off my back, that was the last time I'd accept treatment for nearly three decades. I took my anorexia underground.

CHAPTER 26

For many years I could predict exactly how my body would respond to restriction. I knew what I needed to do to drop a few pounds. And now, I don't.

Since leaving the day hospital program, I've been restricting my calories and exercising in a way that wastes much of my time and energy. I even bought a new food scale to make sure that my estimates weren't wrong. And my weight has hardly budged. I am working out more and eating less, but my body won't play ball.

There were a few recent days of more severe, more intense restriction, and that worked a little, but it didn't feel worth it (is that how regular people feel about dieting? I kind of get it!). To not really eat at all, you have to spend a whole lot of time *thinking* about food. I had forgotten about that. My happiest moment of the day can't be on the scale in the morning. And if I keep it up—the more severe restriction—it will be. I won't have much else left. The restriction will get easier, and I'll stop getting hungry, but I won't be able to go out for dinners or drink wine or get frozen yogurt with my kids. I'll be preoccupied and tired and cold all the time. And not fun. No one is fun when they are starving (not even you, Victoria Beckham). That's not the life I want.

But I really, really want my body to prove to me that it's broken. I want to lose a few pounds and then go back to recovery. I want proof that if I end up fat and sad at the end of all of this,

I don't have to stay there. I need an escape hatch, but one big enough that I can fit through it if I gain a few too many pounds.

So now, my body and I are in a huge fight.

Though there is a strong possibility that I'm the one being a dick.

My body didn't drop dead despite the starvation and the water-loading and the diet pills and the caffeine pills and the short-lived bout of laxative and ipecac abuse in middle school (I'd read an article about what had killed Karen Carpenter—cardiotoxicity brought on by ipecac abuse—and naturally, I took this information as a diet tip in the same vein as "drink lots of water" and sought out the miracle skinny drug that had given her a heart attack). I've never even had a cavity. I never lost my hair. Or my looks, really. And then, this poor, sad, abused body gave me three beautiful, healthy children (one of them can be an a-hole when she's overtired but that's surely related to her paternal gene pool). Maybe now this body is trying to protect me. Maybe if I'd lost the weight I've been hoping to lose, it would be too seductive, and I'd never want to go back to recovery.

Being in this place of medium-restriction and no substantial weight loss has made me so angry at this body. I've been calling it fat and disgusting and punishing it with exercise, despite pain signals and exhaustion. I've been ignoring the hunger signals that it just started sending again in the last couple of years. I've been skipping lunches in order to have dinner with friends and skipping dinners in order to have wine (in those cases my body gets back at me via hangover, so we're even on that front). I'm repulsed by the fat on legs that have healed from fractures three separate times, despite never having been given a day of rest.

On reflection I know that I would never be as mean to anyone as I have been to my body.

But hang on.

Am I my body?

How does that even work?

How is it that I feel bad for abusing my body when I think of it as separate from me—as an innocent victim in this war against myself—but that I feel okay punishing *myself*? Do I really hate myself that much? I feel like I need to find the answer to that rather than continue to take all this anger out on my body. Maybe—probably—we are the same.

CHAPTER 27

Monday January 6, 2020

To do, 2.0

- Get rid of new food scale
- Get rid of new bathroom scale
- Stop fucking buying fucking scales
- Stop walking so much
- Stop thinking about not walking
- Be okay with all of the not-walking
- Stop using the elliptical machine
- Stop thinking about not using the elliptical machine
- Be okay with all of the not using the elliptical machine
- Get calories back up to where they were eight weeks ago
- Stop counting calories
- Stop skipping meals
- Eat challenging foods
- Stop body checking
- Seriously. Stop body checking
- Remember that your thigh gap is meaningless
- Also, stop looking at your thigh gap (because that's body checking, which you are stopping).

- – Recommit to recovery
- – Stop being an asshole to your body
- – Remember that your body is not the enemy
- – Schedule lobotomy

CHAPTER 28

Tuesday

9 a.m. I vow to stop being so awful to my body.

1 p.m. I call the day program coordinator and leave one more message saying that I'd like to try the program again.

Wednesday

10:30 a.m. Coordinator calls me back and offers me a spot for that coming Tuesday. If I say no, I need to go back on the list, which will be about a year's wait. She tells me I have until 2 p.m. to let her know.

10:40 a.m. Call my husband and get sent to voicemail. I start furiously texting my friends.

10:45 a.m. Decide that I'm definitely not doing it.

10:46 a.m. Decide that I'm definitely doing it.

10:47 a.m. Decide that I'm definitely not doing it.

10:48 a.m. Decide that I'm definitely doing it.

10:49 a.m. Decide that I'm definitely not doing it.

10:53 a.m. Decide that I might do it.

11:30 a.m. My husband calls me back, and we discuss logistics of childcare and canceling our three-week family vacation.

11:45 a.m.–1 p.m. Three of the four close friends I've told about the offer furiously text me their opinions (they are all keen on me doing it). Kirsten chooses not to opine.

1 p.m. My husband calls to tell me that we can get credit for our flights.

1:50 p.m. Decide it makes no sense and that I definitely can't do the program right now.

2:10 p.m. Call the coordinator back and say I would rather take a spot after my trip. She says it's now or never and gives me until noon the next day to decide. She wants me to take the spot. I thank her for the extension.

2:10 p.m.–12:45 a.m. Decide I'm definitely not doing it. Fuck her and her extension.

12:47 a.m. Kevin texts and says I should definitely do it. He gives some pretty compelling reasons.

4:47 a.m. Decide to do it.

Thursday

9:10 a.m. Leave a very long rambly message for the coordinator with Kevin and Neil's parrot squawking in the background.

9:20 a.m. She calls me back. I take the spot.

CHAPTER 29

Walking back into the hospital is hard. None of the women I'm expecting are still there. They've all dropped out. I don't know if that says something about the illness or the program or the way they decorate the room (there really is too much beige), but not seeing any of them there, even the annoying ones, is very demoralizing.

The new group I'm with is younger, although there are two women around my age. They refer to each other as "girls," which is really what most of them are. They teach me about TikTok (it's like if Instagram and YouTube had a baby?). "Vogue" comes on the radio during a meal, and none of them know it's a Madonna song. Or who Madonna is. One girl has just transferred out of the children's hospital and cries constantly at the injustice of being kicked out because she just turned eighteen, and because she misses her friends, and talking to sixteen-year-olds, and because she was up too late at a sleepover on the weekend.

I learn they are all bulimic. We will spend hours a day talking about purging. And bingeing. And bingeing and purging. And why it's bad (spoiler: stomach acid should really stay in your stomach). I can't relate.

One girl dominates the conversation and talks only about aesthetics—Spanx, false eyelashes, make-up. How important they are to her. How she feels when she misplaces those things.

Why she needs them. How she feels without them. How wonderful they are. I wonder if this could really be all she cares about, and if anyone else is as angry and embarrassed listening to her drone on about things most men would never waste a millisecond thinking about.

I feel old and misunderstood and alone.

Because my admission into the program this time was so last-minute, my week one menu has been chosen entirely without my input. I am given egg salad for lunch and struggle not to gag as I eat it, and then I struggle to spell the word "sandwich" for the purposes of my food log (sandwhich looks less strange in cursive than you'd expect). This time no one tells me I have to drink the fruit cocktail juice, I already know. I also use all of the probably- radioactive orange salad dressing.

My first dinner is zucchini casserole, which I find hilariously fitting. I feel like I am being tested, either by the team, or the universe.

After dinner I fill out my log (SAD, ANGRY, ANXIOUS, SCARED), and we go around the table to talk about how we felt at the meal.

A woman (she is one of two who are about my age) says she's uncomfortable with people talking about "*behaviors*" at the table because it's "*triggering.*" The nurse practitioner charged with supervising the meal says she didn't notice that anyone had done that. And then the woman says it was me. I wrack my brain, trying to figure out what she's talking about. Finally, it clicks. Incredulous, I say, "Wait. Are you referring to the story about the sad, toothless, stray cat I had in law school who had been homeless for so long that she couldn't keep food down? Is *that* what you are talking about?"

It was. I hadn't even been talking to her, I'd been talking to the woman next to me. And furthermore, that cat wasn't purging to control her weight; she was *a cat* who had been stray for so long that she couldn't digest food properly. She *was* naturally thin (even under all that fur), but I didn't even mention that or all the exercise she got chasing shadows (so much cardio! All the triggers!).

Maybe I should have apologized, but I could not. Instead, I said her reaction was completely ridiculous (which is basically the same as an apology?). And that's how I made an enemy on my very first day.

Having an enemy in the group is not ideal, and I try to make amends the next day, apologizing for not taking her cat complaint more seriously, even though I can't possibly imagine that she is taking it seriously either, given that she brings up both exercise and human vomit the next day at meals and seems fine and pretty not-triggered. Maybe she can tell my apology isn't as sincere as it should have been. Maybe it's because I also mention Kevin and Neil's bird's exceptionally low body fat percentage and very toned bird-body (under the feathers) at the next meal (actually I don't do this, I only fantasize about it), but it becomes painfully obvious to me that not only will we never be friends, but that she has it out for me.

I overhear her talking about me and see her rolling her eyes when I talk. She accuses me of following her to the bathroom when I'd left the room first, and she tells me she's not the only one who has a problem with me (though that wounds me initially, I'm now quite certain that the person she named likes me). It's all very juvenile and ridiculous—and exceptionally hurtful. Not being liked is really hard for me. Being overtly disliked is incredibly painful. I try to make amends. I smile at her when I catch her staring. I nod along with her in groups, hoping she will recognize it for what it is—a sign that we are more alike than not. But her cruelty continues. I've come to understand that none of it is about me. I listen to her talk in group therapy, and at meals, and it becomes obvious to me that I have the things she wants—friends, a husband, kids, a busy and satisfying life outside the disorder. And that really, really bothers her.

Those things also make me feel like I'm not sick enough to be in the program.

Most of the other patients have less to lose. Their lives have been reduced to their illnesses. They aren't giving up time away from kids, and friends, and volunteer work, and canceling a family vacation to be there.

And yet, even though I'm not scary-skinny or throwing up after meals or so ill that I can't maintain relationships, I am like them. The eighteen-year-old cries at the lunch table minutes after I've cried by myself in the bathroom. The makeup-obsessed girl admits to needing all of those things to feel accepted. The mean girl talks about how she feels unworthy of food and not special enough to be in a bigger body.

Our eating disorders are a great equalizer.

When it comes down to it, we are the same.

CHAPTER 30

Week 2

Monday

12:30 p.m. I have permission to leave the program after lunch owing to prearranged travel. I have never been happier to leave any place, ever.

Tuesday

So glad not to be there. I feel like I'm on probation.

Wednesday

7:30 a.m. I'm at the airport waiting to fly back home. Am thrilled by every possible delay. Wonder if I can convince someone in security to detain me. Sadly, I am a white woman in my forties. No detention for me.

9:20 a.m. Land. Can't find my car. Enjoy walking around the Park 'N Fly in subarctic temperatures while dragging carry-on luggage. Am a little disappointed when my car turns up. Was hoping to kill some time filing a police report.

9:40 a.m. Park in the hospital lot. Feel my heart drop into my stomach. Contemplate not going in.

9:45 a.m. Exit elevator. Pretend to be turning left into rehab area. When elevator doors close, make a sharp ninety-degree turn and rush through doors labeled MENTAL HEALTH.

9:48 a.m. Walk into some kind of group therapy session. Everyone stares as I sit down. They are talking about an exciting and innovative therapeutic tool: pro/con lists. Wish I hadn't come back.

6:00 p.m. Freedom! I drive in traffic, drop my car off at home and rush to a school council meeting that I'm chairing. I don't get a chance to see my kids.

9 p.m. Go out for drinks. Find it hard to be present with my friends. One asks if I'm upset with her because I'm quieter than usual. Tell her I'm just tired and reflect on how much I must usually talk if being a little quiet makes people think I'm angry at them.

Thursday

7 a.m. Two of my kids have fevers, and all three are tired and cranky. I decide to keep them all home from school.

8:30 a.m. Cleaner arrives. I ask her if she can watch the kids while I leave the house for a bit. She is free until 1.

8:44 a.m. On my way to the hospital, realize I haven't told the school that my kids won't be in. Text the office admin at a red light.

8:48 a.m. I'm pulled over by a cop who accuses me of texting and driving

8:48 a.m. Realize a ticket will make me late for the program. Which wouldn't be a big deal but for the fact that I'm also leaving early because of my sick kids. And because I was late the day before. And missed the day before that.

8:48 a.m. A sudden flood of adrenaline proceeds to temporarily paralyze my frontal lobe.

8:48 a.m. Tell the cop he's wrong and that in fact I was texting while *stopped*. Police officers like it when people are feisty and argumentative.

8:48 a.m. He tells me he saw me.

8:49 a.m. Tell him that he didn't. I also tell him I'm on my way to the hospital, and I have sick kids at home

8:49 a.m. He tells me I'm lying and asks to see my phone.

8:49 a.m. I tell him *he's* lying and accidentally drop my phone.

8:49 a.m. He is angry and presumes I dropped it on purpose.

8:49 a.m. I reach to pick it up and try to determine whether I should change the screen to *Maps*, so that when he looks he'll see I really do have the hospital programmed in.

8:49 a.m. I go for it. Yet another error in judgment.

8:49 a.m. He sees I've changed the screen and is livid. He puts it back to my texts. I tell him to go ahead and check the time stamps on the texts, maintaining he's wrong and that I wasn't driving and texting (because I wasn't).

8:50 a.m. Unlike most police officers who are known for their love of constructive criticism, he doesn't enjoy being told that he's wrong for the second time in two minutes. He asks to see my license.

8:50 a.m. Start looking through my very full and very messy wallet in search of my license. I'm reminded that I have gift cards for La Senza, Gap, and Toys R Us. No license to be found.

8:53 a.m. He snaps "Do you even have a license?" I snap back "Of course I do!"

8:53 a.m. Pour the contents of my wallet onto the passenger seat. I find three more gift cards (yay!) but no license. Right before panic sets in, I remember using it the day before for ID at the airport. It's in my jacket pocket.

8:55 a.m. Hand my license to my new best friend. He grabs it and walks to his car.

8:58 a.m. Can't decide whether I'm allowed to use my phone.

9:04 a.m. Boredom sets in, and I decide I must be because I'm parked. And also that it would be a hilarious irony if I got another ticket for texting while parked while waiting for a ticket.

9:05 a.m. Text Kirsten to tell her what happened. She texts me back to say she's at a red light, and that she's going to put her phone away.

9:10 a.m. Police officer finally comes back with a ticket. He is giving me the stiffest penalty. Three demerit points and a three-day license suspension, which will come into effect when I pay the $626 fine.

9:10 a.m. Tell him he's being unfair, that I have kids and need my license. He says that it would have been worse if he'd had to call my kids to tell them that I was dead because I was texting and driving. I tell him that wouldn't have happened because "I WASN'T TEXTING AND DRIVING."

9:11 a.m. He storms off and I drive off.

9:30 a.m. Get off the elevator and pretend to look like a confused cleaner coming in for a job interview as I open the doors reading MENTAL HEALTH.

9:35 a.m. Find the social worker and tell her what happened and that I can't stay. She examines the ticket and tells me to go fill out my menus for the week, and that I can go after that.

10:20 a.m. Leave the hospital and spend the rest of the morning trying to deal with my ticket. Then I go home and deal with my sick children. I'm still quite happy not to be at the program.

Friday

9:00 a.m. Get off the elevator and pretend to be a very keen volunteer with a background in theater coming in to do improv with the patients. I pretend to be running lines to myself and realize too late that probably makes me look *more* like a mental patient and drop my character as I quickly walk through the doors reading MENTAL HEALTH.

9:05 a.m. Another group. More vomit-talk. I feel naive for thinking that becoming a mom would be the reason I have to constantly hear about bodily fluids, but that around adults I would be mostly safe.

9:44 a.m. A woman who has been away for a couple days comes in and takes a seat. The facilitator asks if she has been ill. The woman responds with a simple "Nope." I'm in awe of how cool she is.

10:20–11:50 a.m. Free time. I get my nails done down the street. They do a so-so job.

12:00 p.m. Unsupervised brown bag lunch in the cafeteria. I hear that Mean Girl has a blind date scheduled for the weekend. I wonder if love will make her nicer. I think of what it did for Lady Macbeth and am hopeful.

12:45 p.m. Freedom

Week 3

Monday

7:00 a.m. Having been sick all weekend with whatever my kids had, I wake up still ill. I contemplate not going in but decide to rally because I've already missed so many days.

8:59 a.m. Get off the elevator and pretend to be someone with a cough (which I conveniently have) looking for a walk-in clinic. Walk through the doors reading MENTAL HEALTH pretending I'm only going in to ask for directions.

9:00 a.m. Weekend review. When we go around the circle I admit (having been persuaded by Kirsten that it's the right thing to do) that I'm still struggling with exercise, and that even though I'm doing less, I haven't stopped. Others admit to bingeing and purging over the weekend. Mean Girl says she spent Friday afternoon cross country skiing.

9:43 a.m. Someone casually strolls in late. No apologies, she takes out her headphones and sits down.

9:55 a.m. Another woman who is consistently late arrives. The group facilitator doesn't say anything to either of them.

11:15 a.m. Drive myself and one other patient to the agreed-upon meeting place for the bi-weekly restaurant meal. I'm sad that it's a mediocre chain restaurant I'd never normally frequent but also voted for it precisely because it's a mediocre chain restaurant that no one I know frequents.

11:30 a.m. Waitress acts like I'm the first adult patron ever to order a glass of soy milk, then ask someone else at the table for permission to get a soy latte and change my order.

11:45 a.m. Waitress finally finishes taking our drink orders. She clearly thinks we're all prisoners given that none of us appear able to make a decision without permission. I push the thought that she might think that we are MENTAL PATIENTS out of my mind. I try to think of some prisoner-like things to have ready to say when she comes back to take our food orders and regret having stopped watching *Orange is the New Black* at the end of season one.

11:48 a.m. We are told exactly what we are and aren't allowed to order. I can't find a way to work the term "slammer" or "day parole" into my French toast ordering.

12:06 p.m. My meal arrives. I refuse to add syrup to the French toast, citing the tried-and-true "it's already covered in powdered sugar" argument. It works. I can't believe it.

12:25 p.m. I'm told that I'm done after I eat one more piece of what is clearly garnish. I think for the thirty thousandth time that month how infantilizing all of it is and use all my energy not to cry, or bolt.

12:45–2:45 p.m. More downtime. Go to a nearby beauty supply store and buy expensive shampoo and conditioner that promises both luster *and* shine. Then I browse in Walmart.

2:45 p.m. Snack (are they fucking kidding me?).

3:00 p.m. We are told there is going to be a meeting with the whole team. This is unscheduled and unprecedented. We are all in trouble.

3:05 p.m. The whole team marches in and take seats at the front of the room. The head of the program, who I have never met but I've heard is terribly mean and unsympathetic, does all the talking. She lives up to her reputation. Lady Voldemort says people are coming in late too frequently and are missing too many days (all of this is not not-true but her delivery could use some work).

3:08 p.m. One of the chronic latecomers comments that there is no individual therapy, and she feels like her issues are not being addressed. Lady Voldemort harshly tells her that's the way it is, and if she doesn't like it that she's welcome to discharge herself. She looks at the rest of us with steely eyes and says we are *all* welcome to discharge ourselves. The woman-girl starts to cry. She will discharge herself the next morning.

Tuesday

8:20 a.m. Look for the heaviest sweater I own and tear my room apart in search of the heavy leather belt I bought my second year of undergrad. Put them on.

8:40 a.m. Grab two-liter bottle of club soda to drink en route to the hospital. Take a swig at every red light. Realize I look like a total weirdo. Weigh-in panic outweighs concerns about how weird I look.

9:00 a.m. Arrive at the hospital. I have to pee.

9:04 a.m. Get off the elevator and pretend to be someone looking for a bathroom as I quickly walk through the doors reading MENTAL HEALTH. I am so in-character that I'm temporarily comforted by the fiction there is a bathroom in my immediate future.

9:07 a.m. Listen to two bulimic co-patients discuss how they haven't had breakfast yet because they are worried about the weigh-in (being upset by high numbers). Take a swig of water and cross my legs.

9:40 a.m. Weigh-in. Weight is down by a pound. Tell the dietician it's because I'm sick and dehydrated. Hope I don't cough or sneeze, which will prove how very well-hydrated I am.

9:41 a.m. Dietician says she's going to add three extra items per day to my meal plan. I confess that in addition to being sick I'm still exercising and promise to stop if she gives me one more week. Also promise a huge gain for the upcoming week. Feel like a sleazy bookie, but it works.

9:41 a.m. Dietitian agrees to add only one extra item and says she will add three more if I haven't gained a sufficient amount of weight by next week's weigh-in. The truth is my metabolism has clearly sped up, because I'm eating all the food and I'm not exercising enough to account for the weight loss. I'm so confused by all of it and wish that I could talk about it honestly with someone.

3:30 p.m. I'm sent home because they deem me too sick to be there. I cannot believe my good fortune (is a cough, sore throat, nasal congestion, achiness, headache, chills and hoarse voice really all it takes?) but I also don't know what to do with myself because I feel bad showing up at home too early as my sitter has arranged her afternoon around picking up my kids. Run some errands and go for a long walk.

Wednesday

8:45 a.m. Leave my house without my oldest child, who is refusing to go to school.

9:02 a.m. Get off the elevator and look only at the floor, adhering to the old "if I can't see them, they can't see me" adage, and don't look up until after I've walked through the doors reading MENTAL HEALTH.

9:05 a.m. Arrive late only to learn that yet another session has been canceled. There is a note to go to a room in a different area of the ward for an impromptu group to be run by the nurse practitioner.

9:08 a.m. Get to the new room and realize that it's directly across from my neighbor's office. I look in the other direction, counting on the if-I-can't-see-them-they-can't-see-me rule for the second time that morning.

9:10 a.m. It's a slide show. About throwing up. Pictures of intestines and an esophagus. I feel like I know where this slide show is headed (forcing yourself to vomit multiple times daily is bad). I pull out my phone and text the school to let them know that my son is still at home.

9:15 a.m. More slides. Vomiting repeatedly is also bad for your teeth. I respond to a text from my unbelievably sweet and thoughtful friend Cali, who is very keen on going to my house and dragging my son to school and I tell her to please not bother.

9:15 a.m. I am admonished for texting. Annoyed, I tell the nurse that the slides don't apply to me; I can text and listen at the same time; *and* that I'm dealing with an urgent situation with one of my kids who doesn't want to go to school. I don't point out that there are two other people texting, but they are sitting farther away from her.

9:15 a.m. She tells me to go deal with the issue outside. I leave the room and get as far away from my neighbor's office as I can (I take the stairs four floors down and walk toward the cafeteria).

9:20–9:50 a.m. Call my son multiple times trying to persuade him to go to school. I also browse in the lobby a little. There is a vendor selling jewelry. Spend $70 on earrings for my daughters. Apple Pay has changed my life.

9:52 a.m. Arrive back for the end of the slide show. Feel pretty good about having missed it and sad for everyone who didn't (the staff can't actually think you can *fix* people by showing them scary slides?). Tell co-patients I'm not going to talk to any of them on the way out because I need to run past my neighbor's office. They seem to understand.

12:00 p.m. Lunch.

12:20 p.m. We go around the circle to discuss how we feel. I say my pizza slice was twice the size of everyone else's and it felt unfair. I'm harshly reprimanded for saying that. It's the nurse who did the slide show, and she's holding a grudge.

4:45 p.m. Say I'm feeling too ill to stay for dinner. I still have my cough and figure I might as well use it to my advantage. Freedom is mine.

Thursday

12:00 p.m. It's my first "self-serve lunch," which means we all are having the same thing, served from large communal platters. Except it's chicken, and I don't eat meat. I run down to buy some fish from the cafeteria.

12:05 p.m. I also have rice, salad, bread and butter, and milk. I learn that self-serve is a misnomer, because it's self-serve with the dietician looking over your shoulder telling you how much to serve yourself. And you always need to serve yourself more.

12:20 p.m. Dessert is a very large pan of date squares sent up from the cafeteria. The dietician cuts the entire pan into eight squares and hands us each a date square the size of a dessert plate. We are all in shock. I get up and leave the room. The dietician tells me if I don't eat the date square I'm out of the program. I tell her I need some air. I honestly don't know if I'm going to come back.

12:25 p.m. I go downstairs and text Kirsten, Kevin, and Neil, and tell them I'm on the cusp of leaving. I'm not going to make the same mistake I did last time, which was storming out without telling anyone.

12:26 p.m. Kirsten seems exasperated, like she has nothing left to say. She does her best, but I sense she's unimpressed with me and my lack of motivation to save myself. I'm embarrassed for having interrupted her already-stressful day with a dessert crisis.

12:35 p.m. Kevin and Neil text me back and tell me I need to just do it. Kevin says to call him and convinces me that if I don't eat the stupid date square the decision to leave will be made for me, and that I will be sad and regretful, exactly like I was the last time. He says the pain of the date square is smaller than the pain and guilt I'll feel if this is how it ends. His words resonate, and I'm overcome with gratitude, again. I feel so unlucky to have to go back in to eat a date square the size of a small puppy, but I feel so ridiculously lucky to have such incredible friends.

1:00 p.m. I go back in and say I'm ready to eat the date square. Everyone is still there and has moved onto menu planning. The dietician wordlessly serves me the last date square.

1:05 p.m. It's worse than I thought. It takes a long time because breathing and chewing and crying simultaneously prove very difficult. I wonder if anyone has ever died of having aspirated a date square. I also wonder if death by date square would be better or worse than how I'll feel after having eaten the date square. The room is very quiet. Everyone seems panic-stricken as we fill out our menus for the following week and choose the next self-serve lunch

(Mean Girl insists we order chicken again; I can't be bothered to argue. I just make sure dessert isn't anything served in squares. We settle on pie).

2:30 p.m. We all pile into cars to get groceries for a lunch we're going to make the following Monday. I can say with certainty that group grocery shopping with a bunch of not-friends and a dietician whom you feel nothing but anger toward is less fun than shopping with overtired, hungry, sick, yelly children.

3:30 p.m. We arrive back at the hospital and are free until dinner. I can't stop thinking about the date square. I go for a walk despite some heavy snow.

5:30 p.m. Dinner. We eat in silence. Everyone is still pretty traumatized.

5:50 p.m. We go around the table, and there are tears. A couple of women are worried they are going to go home and binge/purge. I know I'm going to go home and exercise. The date squares were a colossal failure, but no staff member is willing to admit it or take responsibility.

8:30 p.m. Do a vigorous workout on my home elliptical machine after my kids are in bed. I can still taste the date square.

Friday

8:58 a.m. See some rocks on the ground on the way in, and they remind me of crumb and butter topping, I'm flooded with guilt and nausea. Date square PTSD is apparently a thing.

9:01 a.m. Get off the elevator and just walk in the doors reading MENTAL HEALTH. I'm sad, and angry, and dejected.

10:30 a.m. It's my week for a "discharge planning meeting" with the social worker. We spend the time talking about my ambivalence about the program and what I should do.

12:00 p.m. Unsupervised cafeteria lunch day. We eat the lunches we packed at home. Someone says that the dietician (who is new to the job, Socks and Sandals retired a few weeks earlier) admitted to the date squares having been a mistake—that they weren't meant to have been as large. I also hear a rumor of post-date-square purging. I ask for no details on that front but do say I'm furious with the dietician.

12:02 p.m. Mean Girl gives me a dirty look and asks us to stop talking about it because it's *triggering*. I can't even.

12:30 p.m. Freedom.

Week 4

Monday

9:00 a.m. I get off the elevator and pretend to be so distracted that I haven't noticed I'm about to walk through doors reading MENTAL HEALTH, which is certainly not where I am supposed to be. I'm trying to play the part of someone who is very distracted but *definitely* not a patient.

9:15 a.m. Weekend review. Admit that I'm still struggling with exercise but that even though I didn't do zero, I did significantly less than usual/I wanted to. Also talk about some successful food challenges. Two patients admit to having purged, one admits to self-harm, and Mean Girl says she went dancing, skating, and cross-country skiing (exercise-palooza!). She also claims that exercise and her eating disorder are in no way connected. I try not to let my eyes roll all the way into my head.

10:00 a.m. Another canceled group. More free time. I ask the dietician if I can talk to her. She tells me to come by at 10:30.

10:45 a.m. Dietician finally shows up at her office. I follow her in, close the door and let out my frustration around #Datesquaregate. I'm livid and I'm not trying to hide it.

10:55 a.m. She tells me part of recovery is being able to eat whatever is put in front of me. I tell her that no one should be expected to go from never having eaten a date square to being forced to eat what amounts to four in one sitting, after a full meal. We are both very agitated.

10:58 a.m. We leave her office together to join the other patients. We walk down the hall in silence.

11:00 a.m. We are making a lunch of tilapia, couscous, broccoli, and banana bread. I'm in charge of the banana bread and pretend I'm on a cooking show. Everyone is having fun and is engaged with my silly cooking show, except Mean Girl, who rolls her eyes and whispers something. I ask her if she has something to say, and if she'd like to share it with everyone. We are almost the same age, but I'm a *mom* and I've had it with her attitude. She shakes her head no. I return to putting on my show.

11:20 a.m. I watch as butter is smeared all over the fish. I try not to outwardly panic.

12:00 a.m. We sit down to the lunch we've made. It actually tastes really good.

12:25 p.m. I'm served a piece of warm banana bread. A recipe I make so frequently for my family that I know it by heart. It's the first time I've ever had a piece. It's excellent. Everyone wants the recipe.

12:35 p.m. I can't believe I ate all of that stuff and liked it. I had fish with butter! And a whole piece of cake! When I fill out my meal log, I circle HAPPY in addition to the usual ANXIOUS, WORRIED, SCARED.

12:45 p.m. Text Cali, who knew how worried I was about lunch, to say it was the best meal I've had in the three weeks I've been in the program. I feel something that reminds me of happiness.

3:00 p.m. Another group.

3:20 p.m. Lady Voldemort pops her head in and summons someone to come talk to her. I haven't seen her since she yelled at everyone the week prior.

3:30 p.m. Patient comes back sobbing.

3:31 p.m. Lady Voldemort summons Mean Girl.

3:40 p.m. Mean Girl comes back wiping her red-rimmed eyes.

3:41 p.m. Lady Voldemort calls my name next. I follow her out of the room.

3:43 p.m. She introduces herself and in the same breath tells me she's heard I "have been having a hard time adjusting to the program." I nod.

3:44 p.m. She tells me I can't be in the program because I'm not committed enough, and that it's my last day.

3:45 p.m. I ask if her decision is final.

3:46 p.m. She says that it is. I say that I'm shocked and ask why I'm being kicked out without any warning.

3:47 p.m. She says she heard that I am exercising. And that I walked out of the room during a meal (she is referring to the date square). I remind her that I also came back *into* the room and ate a date square the size of a litter of newborn kittens. And that if I could completely abstain from exercise I wouldn't need the program. And that I've cut down, and that I'm trying my best. And that I was honest about it, when my instinct was not to be. I remind her that I've had an eating disorder for thirty-five years (which is almost twice as many years as the youngest person in the program has been alive).

3:48 p.m. She tells me there is no doubt in her mind that I'm "very ill." But also, that I can't stay. She says I can reapply when I'm ready.

3:49 p.m. I stand up and walk to the door. She says I can stay until the end of the day. I almost laugh out loud picturing a universe where I'm already kicked out, but choose to stay for dinner.

3:52 p.m. I go back into the room, gather my things and leave. I don't say goodbye.

3:56 p.m. Shellshocked, I walk around the ward looking for another staff member to talk to but can't find anyone.

4:04 p.m. Finally, I see the psychologist who was facilitating the last group on her way out the door. She's wearing her coat and has her bag with her. I ask again if the decision is final. She says it is. I ask if she can give me some reasons. She says she's in a rush, but that I can call Lady Voldemort in the morning if I want more information.

4:15 p.m. I text my husband and a few friends to tell them what happened. Two of them call me. I sit in the parking lot on the phone until well after five.

5:45 p.m. I walk into my house on time for dinner. I can't believe it's over. I don't know what to eat.

CHAPTER 31

I was almost fired from my very first part-time job at Dairy Queen at the age of fourteen for refusing to give a customer plastic spoons with a to-go order, mere days after I'd told another customer he had taken too many napkins. (I had recently joined the Environmental Youth Alliance and was taking my job as ambassador very seriously). There was no question in my boss's mind who the subject of the complaints was when they came in. I got off with a warning and a promise that I'd stop telling customers that it was *their generation that was destroying the planet* and went on to work there for four years.

I was almost fired from multiple waitressing jobs in high school and university. I refused to write things down, and as a result was easily flustered when a rush came in and frequently got orders wrong and then tried to convince patrons that whatever I brought them was what they wanted. I also dropped things sometimes.

I was let go from a job working the front desk of a hotel the summer after my second year of undergrad. I had just quit smoking and was caught with giant wads of gum in my mouth multiple times daily and was given more warnings than I deserved. As soon as the summer bustle calmed down, I was the first to be sent packing.

I was nearly kicked out of my pre-professional ballet company at the age of sixteen because all of my bones were visible, and I was awful to look at in a leotard. I was hospitalized shortly after the concerned director called my mom, so they didn't need to kick me out, and I decided on my own not to return. I was tired of the classes and didn't have the desire—or the talent—to take that much farther.

But never ever have I ever been fired from a voluntary medical program. I didn't even know that could happen.

It was no secret to anyone that I was ambivalent about being there. I wrote a pro/con list about quitting the program and brought it to a group.

Though I still showed up every day. I showed up when I was sick. I showed up when I got a ticket. I participated in groups and did the homework and made friends with girls half my age (and also made one arch nemesis). Most importantly, I was honest with them, about the exercise, and the fear, and the ambivalence, and I was penalized for it. I was fired without warning or an explanation.

It makes for a funny enough anecdote I guess, but also a sad one.

Friends said I should complain. To whom? And what would I say? I am an actual mental case. And when the doctors come back with something about me being not-ready, they would be right. But if I had no ambivalence, and if I had been completely ready, I don't think I would have needed the program in the way I did.

Last I heard, out of my group of eight, two of us were kicked out and four more dropped out. Those are not very good odds. Though it wasn't a very good program, and I'm sad about that too.

CHAPTER 32

THINGS I LEARNED IN MY BULLSHIT DAY HOSPITAL PROGRAM, DESPITE THE FACT IT WAS A BULLSHIT PROGRAM

1. Eating tons and tons didn't cause me to gain weight. In fact, I lost weight, which is a sure sign my metabolism is suppressed when I undereat.
2. Date squares are really disgusting but buttered fish is pretty good.
3. I can eat more than I'm comfortable with and survive.
4. I can eat things I don't like and survive.
5. I know more about how to recover than I thought I did.
6. I can do really hard things.
7. The hospital needs a recycling program.
8. Ultimately, I am responsible for my own recovery.

CHAPTER 33

Introduction

I'm writing this plan for someone who definitely isn't me. It's for someone who has an eating disorder and exercise addiction that looks a lot like mine, but she is definitely not me because if I were writing my own plan, I could not possibly be objective.

Patient Profile: Mid-to-late forties, has stopped formal exercise, but still feels driven to walk a lot. Compares herself to others when it comes to movement, still has many fear foods, counts calories. Not severely underweight but below target BMI, as set by medical professionals. Has naturally straight hair that never requires blow-drying, kids who listen, and a super-clean house at all times. Never yells. (See? Absolutely. not. me.)

Food

Calories: You need to stop counting calories. You've done a good job resisting the urge to measure and weigh food, but we all know that eyeballing things to the gram is your superpower (maybe you can look for a job as a drug dispenser when this is all over—drug dealing can be very lucrative, and precision is important). You need to start using different bowls. And getting other people to portion your food when possible, including restaurant meals. You need to think about other things when the urge to count arises. Never look up the things you don't know. It's going to make you feel like your head is going to explode, but don't give in. Recite the alphabet backward, count split ends (which you probably don't have because you don't blow dry your naturally pin-straight hair). You know the calories in almost all the things but try to ignore them. Don't tally them up as part of a daily total. Don't. give. in. You will use the excuse that you want to make sure you hit your baseline, and some days maybe you won't quite get there, but as you continue to eat challenging foods and really pay attention to your hunger, this should happen with reduced frequency.

Fear Foods: You need to keep challenging fear foods—plan for at least three a week, but when the opportunity arises to try an unplanned one, take it. Have each fear food at least three times, and if after three times it's still scary, keep going. And once it's in, keep it in your diet, don't let it get scary again. One-off challenges are dumb. This isn't a game show, this is your life. And for fuck's sake, don't compensate by moving more or eating less. This wastes the challenge. Food is just food. And fear food is just food with a bad reputation.

Hunger: Eat to satiety when you are hungry. Even if it feels like too much. Even if it's midnight, and you have already had a snack, or you have already finished a serving that you deem sufficient, or excessive. And also, eat when you aren't hungry. Say yes to things you are offered. Taste the things you are offering others (they might be awful, wouldn't you like to know? Your friends certainly won't tell you). Don't skip meals and snacks just because you have no appetite; that rule gets you into trouble. And pay attention to your body—sometimes hunger presents itself as thinking about food, or irritability, or a headache, it still counts.

Variety: Branch out. Eat what your kids are eating. Eat what your friends are eating. Drink scary cocktails instead of wine sometimes. Accept dinner invitations. And for the love of god, change your breakfast once in a while (tomorrow, for example).

Movement

I mean this in the nicest way possible, but your relationship with movement is really fucked up. This is going to be very hard to hear, but you probably need to stop walking for a while to break the link between exercise and your body shape and size. And also, you need to learn to live with the discomfort of being still. If you were less afraid of dying on the operating table for vanity-related reasons, I'd strongly suggest a cosmetic procedure after which you will be forced to rest to recuperate (and also, maybe that's the wrong message to be sending as we talk about body-acceptance. So nevermind).

You are going to say that it's unfair. And that everyone exercises. And that exercise is healthy and normal. And that the only exercise you do these days is walk, which brings you happiness. You will say that you have already given up so much. But think about how much time you have lost to exercise, and how many afternoons with your kids were dictated by your disorder. Think about all the relationships and fun things you missed out on in university and law school (I mean veterinary school! You didn't go to law school!) because the gym took precedence. Think about what it might feel like to spend a snowy day at home, or a lazy day at the beach, or a long weekend at a cottage, without the pull to move and all. that. guilt.

If you can't commit to a long break, commit to two weeks—just to hit the reset button before it all goes off the rails again.

Think of activities you can do instead. Tell some friends so they can provide support, and keep you company, and not invite you for walks, or tell you about their workouts.

You can also ignore this advice. You can keep doing what you're doing, and maybe you will be okay, as long as you are careful. And as long as you're okay with the idea that you will never be able to fully relax. But your exercise addiction is insidious, and it will probably get very bad again soon.

Another option would be to try to reduce your walking and see how that works. Break rules. Go for shorter walks some days. Change your routes. Stick to a strict daily maximum. Be the one who ends a long walk first. Stop before you're tired. Be completely honest with yourself and everyone around you. Not to be a douchebag about it, but you will probably fail at this. Though you can try it.

Weight

Every single eating disorder professional says that you need to get up to BMI 20. Why can't you do that? It will either help with the noise, or it won't. But also, in order to get to that weight, you will be doing things that are beneficial to your recovery. And maybe that will feel okay. And maybe you will grow boobs. And maybe the unrelenting critical voice in your head won't be as loud and that will allow you to keep going until you get to your natural unsuppressed body weight. Because if you can't do that, you will probably stay stuck.

Friends

You should consider letting more people in. Before you say no, please consider the following:

No one you've told about your ED is no longer your friend (or treats you like you are any crazier than they did before they knew).

Many of the people you have told have been amazing sources of kindness and support.

You worry a lot about what people will think if they notice you gaining weight.

Sometimes hearing about other people's weight-loss plans and exercise regimens sets you back for days.

At best, more people knowing probably means more support and less explaining and more people to reach out to when you want to exercise, but can't. And at worst, it means you can unabashedly give them very, very dirty looks when they tell you about their long runs and the fact they haven't eaten all day.

Mindfulness

Take a class. Watch a seminar. Do a meditation app. Do the mindfulness workbook that I bought two years ago and only opened once—I'll sell it to you (for a very small markup because the first exercise is already done for you). You need to learn how to experience feelings in a different way. You need to know they will pass. That they are just feelings. Mindfulness will help get you there.

Therapy

Find someone you respect. If you want to stick with your current therapist, start giving her the benefit of the doubt. You can't be constantly questioning her judgment and expect to get something out of therapy.

Your Body

It's just a body. It's the least important thing about you. No one likes you or doesn't like you because of how much space there is between your thighs. Do some body-image work. Unpack why being in a small body is so important to you. Remember all the terrible crazy shit you've done to your poor body over the years and cry tears of gratitude for the fact it didn't drop dead when you were starving it and poisoning it, and that it healed over and over when you thoughtlessly injured it, and that it gave you healthy, beautiful children (who are perfectly behaved and who never swear).

Conclusion

So there it is. These are my recommendations. If you take them all and find yourself fat and miserable in a year, well, you can always go back. You have tried everything else. You have tried illness. You have tried denial. You have tried quasi-recovery, and relapsing, and living in this place that looks like wellness but feels like illness. You have tried toe-dipping and stops and starts. You have tried wishing on stars, and dandelions, and birthday candles (on cake that you never eat). So try something new. It's time.

CHAPTER 34

From: Sheri Segal Glick
Subject: Coaching
To: Emily
Date: June 15, 2020, 4:52 p.m.

Hi Emily,

I hope this email finds you well, despite the global pandemic.

I'm writing to see if you would be willing to resume coaching.

I haven't used the elliptical since the first week of April. I stopped of my own volition (the therapist I've been seeing felt like it was okay to keep using it in moderation). It's still in my house but I would be willing to commit to selling it immediately if I started using it again. Right now, I don't feel a pull to use it at all—I used it once, the week I decided to stop, and haven't slipped up since then.

For the first time really, I feel ready to do the things necessary to recover. I'm not measuring any food, I'm mostly eating the same dinners as the kids (and haven't had tofu and broccoli in months), and I've been going through my fear foods list again. Walking is still an issue, as is calorie counting, and my fear of weight gain. I'd like to get past those things.

I found a specialist who does cognitive behavioral therapy mid-March and have been seeing her remotely. Unfortunately, I don't feel like she understands my exercise issues (she thinks the walking will resolve itself, as long as I continue to break rules) or much of anything, really. It feels like I'm paying her to pat me on the head whenever I succeed at a challenge, or to tell me that it isn't my fault when I fail.

I understand why coaching me again might not be something you want to do, but I thought I'd check to see if it's something you might consider, even on a trial basis.

Okay. I'll stop rambling now because this feels awkward.

Yours truly,
Sheri

CHAPTER 35

Quasi-recovery

> qua·si re·cov·ery | | \ ˈkwā- zī ri-ˈkə-və-rē
> plural quasi recoveries
>
> Definition of quasi-recovery

1. the act, process, or an instance of recovering from anorexia only up to a certain point because you are terrified of gaining too much weight.

2. when your healthier looking body makes it look like your head is less fucked, but actually you are just as fucked up—or more fucked up—than before.

See also: fear, denial, semi-recovery

Quasi-recovery is a concept I first heard a few years ago, around the same time a therapist told me I had functional anorexia. They are both weird near-oxymorons, like being told you have a mild case of pregnancy or that you are a thoughtful sociopath.

Quasi-recovery is the place between acute illness and full recovery where a lot of us get stuck. It doesn't mean you are halfway better. It means that you can eat more things, and people don't look at you and immediately presume you have anorexia, but the noise is just as bad. Which is also hard, because your mostly normal-looking body doesn't match your definitively not-normal head.

When I was a teenager, my doctors told my parents that if I got better, I'd always be a little underweight, I'd always be slightly preoccupied with my body, and that my eating would always be a little restrictive. That was how they described *recovery*. Can you imagine someone with type 1 diabetes being given a prognosis along those lines? She might fall into light comas sometimes, and annoying nerve and organ damage might get in the way every once in a while, but otherwise she'll be okay (or, she could learn to monitor her blood sugar and take insulin and lead a normal life).

This is why I mostly presumed I was recovered, until I relapsed. Oh yeah, that happens in quasi-recovery too because you're always on the cusp of falling into a more severe energy deficit. A flu or dental surgery, or in my case nursing my youngest child, can send you into a relapse. I suspect that most people who were as ill as I was, around the same time I was (old people), presumed that quasi-recovery was the best they could do.

But there is a whole generation of people who know exactly what quasi-recovery is and get stuck there anyway. Quasi-recovery isn't merely an affliction of ignorance. It's an affliction of fear.

Quasi-recovery is compliments on your thin frame, as opposed to worry about your emaciated one. It's people asking about your exercise regimen because they want to copy it, and not because they're concerned you're overdoing it. Quasi-recovery is diet culture's first cousin once removed. She's not as pretty or popular as diet culture, but people still let her come to all the parties.

My first twenty years of quasi-recovery were unremarkable owing to my very deep state of denial. There was a time when I thought my behavior was normal. I remember going for lunch with a friend in my twenties and being surprised when she ordered dressing on her salad (and didn't tell them to hold the avocado, chicken, cheese, and bread). I think I presumed that all my slim friends did the same things that I did to stay slim. I thought I was living in Normaland when in fact, I was the mayor of Crazytown.

Trying to climb out of quasi-recovery has been harder than all the years of acute illness and all the years between acute illness and learning that other people don't have a voice in their heads constantly berating them for their food choices (what? Isn't that everyone's inner narrative?). Once I understood these things weren't normal, things got really hard because I also began to understand the things I had missed out on.

Every experience I've ever had has been tainted by anorexia. Every single one. Every relationship, job, trip, date, class, hobby, birthday, wedding, and night out. Every single meal. Pregnancy. Childbirth. Motherhood.

I don't even know who I would have become without it. The idea that I will never be the person I should have become, that I am in fact a half-person whose tastes and choices and preferences were molded by what basically amounts to a parasite is a smidge on the depressing side.

That knowledge isn't enough to block the noise or the fear though. It's just enough to make me feel guilty every time I want to run back to the easy comfort of my eating disorder. Where restriction and over-exercising used to offer me relief, now I feel guilty for doing those things too (intense, opposing double guilt! Add another superpower to my list!) because I see my life ticking by.

I know I'm missing out on lazy holidays and birthday cake and opportunities to engage with the world where I'm not constantly thinking about exercise or tallying up how many calories I've burned or consumed in any given moment. I know that I'm missing warm cookies with my children, and relaxed meals with friends. I'm missing out on being fully present. That should be enough.

But the closer I get to recovering, the louder the noise becomes. The eating disorder is smart and sneaky, and it's not going to just let go. And this place of not-that-sick but not that well would be a pretty easy place to take up permanent residence, especially when the eating disorder tells me that the only thing that can change at this point is my clothing size. In moments of doubt (there are so many) I feel like there is no point in forcing myself to rest or eat scary things because this is as good as it gets. I spend hours a day trying to talk myself out of the certitude that if I give up everything I've worked so hard for (a small body, the illusion of control), I'm destined for a life of fatness and desperate self-loathing.

I sometimes wonder if my life would have been better if I'd managed to stay in an anosognosic state indefinitely. Not being able to go back to the numb comfort of restriction really hurts sometimes.

It takes so much faith to feel this deeply uncomfortable and to keep doing the things that are causing the discomfort. Continuing with recovery stuff when things are mostly okay, and I'm mostly healthy requires faith that all of it will pay off, and that as my body gets bigger, my life will too.

I recently had a thought while eating something particularly scary and unpleasant (you would have loved it, I bet) that if I knew my death was imminent, I wouldn't be wasting all this time doing these things that take me so far out of my comfort zone.

Then later that day it occurred to me that if that were the case, I wouldn't be squandering precious time restricting food and planning exercise and worrying about the shape of my body.

So I keep going.

CHAPTER 36

My exercise addiction started my last year of high school. Before that I mostly hated exercise. I hated phys ed because balls used to hit me in the face as if by magnetic force (also, I was usually talking to the person next to me, not looking for stray volleyballs/soccer balls/softballs/badminton rackets). I hated chasing balls and pucks (what's the point if you aren't a golden retriever? I still don't get it), and running around the track felt exhausting and boring. I remember—even at my most ill—lounging in bed and reading for entire weekend mornings and not once thinking about how many steps I had or hadn't taken.

I have always enjoyed walking—I used to go for long walks with my parents and would frequently choose to walk home over taking the crowded school bus, but exercise was never transactional, until it was. I took dance classes because I enjoyed dancing (well, really performing) but a missed class didn't make me panic.

I can't imagine what my hospitalizations would have felt like if I'd had an exercise component to my anorexia back then. There was so much sitting around in the hospital—not just when we were being punished with bed rest, but as a matter of course. It strikes me as odd given how frequently exercise addiction and eating disorders are linked that none of the other girls I was inpatient with had exercise addictions. We all felt like starving ourselves was a sufficient and effective means of weight control. It also makes me question the validity of the *Adapted to Flee Famine Theory* that has become so popular of late. This theory sets out that anorexia is triggered by an evolutionary response to famine, causing the sufferer to want to move compulsively—or migrate—until food is perceived to be readily available again. Proponents of this theory believe this made it easier for our ancestors to leave depleted environments and keep going until they found food again, thus increasing their chances of survival. I think for this to be true, compulsive movement would have to present in all—or at least most—cases of anorexia.

The fact that I didn't have an exercise addiction was the only reason I was able to have a relatively normal life in middle school and high school (not counting hospitalizations, starvation, and arrhythmias). I had hobbies and friends and an agent and a dance troupe and a theater troupe and a spot on the school improv team and parts in shows and plays. None of this would have been possible if I was also walking five hours a day and going to the gym.

During my last year of high school, I lived in an apartment downtown with two older girls I'd met at my part-time retail job. The line I used with friends was that the cheap basement apartment was closer to the performing arts high school I attended, but the truth was my parents had said if I didn't go back to treatment for my anorexia I had to move out. So I did. Move out that is.

A friend from school (a bulimic model with a huge toothy smile) had joined a gym to stay in shape and loved it, and because I had stopped taking dance classes that year, I decided that maybe I should join the gym too. Memberships were expensive though, and I was in high school, so I asked my parents to buy me one for my birthday. And they obliged.

My obsession with the gym began gradually with daily aerobics classes and sessions on cardio machines, but I could still miss the gym for important things, like rehearsals and schoolwork. By the summer before my first year of undergrad, the addiction had a stranglehold.

I had a little group of gym friends. One was an elite swimmer who had spent her life training for the Olympics and hadn't qualified because of a head cold and a tragically unfortunate fraction of a second. One was a first-year law student who had lost a large amount of weight over the course of the year and was terrified of gaining it back. And one was just your average, garden-variety bulimic teen-model with an exercise addiction. We would spend hours on the cardio machines every day, watching talk shows and chatting to pass the time. I mean, it's fine. A lot of kids go to Europe the summer before undergrad. I walked to Europe, via Stairmaster.

By the time I started university in a new city that fall, there was nothing as important as exercising. Not friends, nor classes, nor hobbies. I never wanted to go to the bars, and when I did, I'd leave early because I had to get up for the gym. Sitting around talking in someone's dorm room or the coffee house on campus felt wasteful when I could be having the same conversation on the treadmill, or at least on a walk.

As a result, I missed out. I didn't forge the deep bonds most people do in university. I did make a few friends—some from my program and some from residence, but the people I saw the most were my gym friends (if your main group of friends is gym friends, and your main meeting place is the gym, you too might have a problem). I had two gym memberships—I got a Y membership because the people running the university gym were under the impression I was too thin and spending too much time there, and kept threatening to suspend my membership or start weighing me. I was very popular at both places (because I was always there and would literally talk to anyone to pass time on the cardio machines). My sweaty, spandex-y gym friends were mostly as crazy as I was. If you want to meet the crazies—or if you are a crazy, to find your people—just look for the group lined up at 6 a.m. waiting for the gym to open every morning.

My sparse group of non-gym friends took me for who I was—a selfish dummy who would always put the gym first. Even my romantic relationships were superficial and undemanding: a sweet, handsome boy who, as it turned out, loved other sweet, handsome boys; a thirty-three-year-old neighbor who was still in love with his ex. The ones who cared about me the most—like a smart, silly engineering student on my floor in residence who chased me all of first and second year, giving me massages, and leaving little gifts and funny poems around my suite—wanted too much of my time, and I pushed them away. They were nice enough and cute enough, but unless you flashed red numbers with estimates of calories burned, I wasn't that into you.

Law school was more of the same. I didn't want to be on the law review or work at the legal aid clinic because those things didn't fit with my workout schedule. I had a part-time job at the Academic Advisory Centre and spent the rest of my time in class or at the gym (gyms. I joined the school gym and kept my Y membership). I had a few friends, and some boyfriends (the only one I stayed with long term was a fitness trainer), but I didn't make any lasting or meaningful friendships or attend most things I was invited to, and eventually people mostly stopped asking, and I didn't care, or notice.

Those years were lost. I didn't have the law school or undergrad experiences I should have. Today, I am filled with regret and sadness for the girl who skipped everything to wake up in the dark and go to the gym.

I could keep writing about how my exercise addiction allowed me to do some truly deplorable things (like the time I refused to get on a plane to meet a serious boyfriend's ailing grandmother because I'd miss two days at the gym). And some regrettable ones (like the hundreds of times I've made my children walk places when we could have driven). And how it morphed over the years from an addiction to the gym, to an addiction to the gym and walking, and now that

I've been able to cut out the gym (and my home cardio machines), mainly to walking. I think the most important part of all of this, is not only did I not know what I was missing, I didn't think I was missing anything.

What might have happened if instead of heading out to the gym at 5:30 every morning I had sometimes stumbled home from the bars with my university suitemates? What would my life have been like if I hadn't abandoned my aspirations because I was so achingly exhausted, or because they got in the way of the gym? I could have practiced representing victims in landlord-tenant disputes (the two-day training at the legal aid clinic got in the way of the gym), or followed up with the agency my hometown agent had called on my behalf (auditions and acting jobs got in the way of the gym), or written for the university newspaper (deadlines got in the way of the gym).

I would have spent more time visiting my grandmother in the last years of her life, rather than only once a week. I hate myself, and the illness for that. It was more important for me to get out for walks with my babies and to keep moving constantly than to sit with someone who loved them (and me) as much as she loved anything in the world. I was so numb and obsessed that I was mostly able to ignore the rising tidal wave of guilt. I will live with that shame and regret and cavernous sorrow forever. It's the worst thing I've ever done.

I squandered all of it. Youth. Passions. Health. Relationships. People. Why didn't I notice?

Today, I have more balance and my addiction is well hidden, except to the people I've told. I have great friends, whom I love. I sit on boards, and do volunteer work, and I take care of my three young children (who are almost definitely going to grow into decent, not-sociopaths, maybe). Despite all of it, Kevin once remarked that I waste a lot of my life walking. And that seemed rich coming from him, who walks and runs and bikes and goes to the gym. But he's right. We are not the same. He never chooses movement over his actual life.

In the moment, the hour-long walk to the store seems like a fine use of my time on a nice day. But then it's an hour back. And it's my whole morning. And I'm not doing that once a week on a truly beautiful day. I'm doing it any time I have anywhere to go, where it's feasible for me to walk. And sometimes it feels amazing. I listen to books and podcasts and catch up with friends on the phone. And sometimes I walk in the cold drizzle, trying to convince myself I had a choice. Some days I meet friends for long walks, and the air is crisp and it smells like burnt fall leaves, or it's cool and damp with fresh wet snow, or hot and sticky with the scent of lilacs and flowering crabapples. And it's perfect. And then they go home and feel I have to keep walking. And the weeks bleed into months, and I've wasted so much of my life walking.

So for now, I frequently have to say no to walks with friends. And I have to drive places and feel lazy and uncomfortable and sorry for myself and shell out for parking (and parking tickets because I'm so bad at parking) so that I don't miss anything else. So that I have the space to write and read and clean out my closets. So that I can pay attention to the world without the blinders of my exercise addiction.

And it feels so unfair. But so do the lost years.

I don't know exactly what I'm missing, but I finally understand it's something I won't see until I make room for it.

CHAPTER 37

I was shopping recently and saw a woman with my old body. Not my body of the very ill years, but my adult body of ten pounds ago. So tiny that even the tiniest size was a little too big. And I was jealous of her. But why? She didn't seem exceptionally happy—or sad. I don't know anything about her. Maybe she's that size because of genetics. Or maybe she made the same choices I did to be in that body.

I don't care if her hair is naturally straight or if she blow dries it.

I don't care if her hair is naturally brown or if she dyes it.

She might be as dumb a rutabaga. Or effortlessly brilliant.

She might be dull and humorless.

Or kind, and careful with her words.

Maybe she stole the clothes she was trying on. Or wore them to take care of a sick relative. Or to accept an award. Or to go to her genital wart removal appointment.

I don't care.

Her body has no bearing on my life.

I don't care

I don't care
    I
        don't.
            care.

(I will say it until I believe it)

(I. don't. care.)

CHAPTER 38

Never Have I Ever

Ordered something off a menu just because I thought it might taste good

Gone a whole day without knowing how many calories I consumed

Spent a whole day in my pyjamas

Stayed home on a snowy or rainy weekend

Stopped eating just because I was full

Not known the exact distance between my thighs

Had an entire day where the thought "you are so fat" didn't go through my head

Watched a show about the Kardashians

CHAPTER 39

This weird thing about a restrictive eating disorder is that sometimes it can feel like something one might want to keep when they are contemplating letting it go.

There are the obvious things, like numbness, and societally approved smallness. Or specialness. People with eating disorders can feel special for having the kind of self-control other people want. Or think they want. Total control over drinking, spending, eating. People say they want it. Though really, they don't. People who are able to show the most restraint, to deprive themselves, to be satisfied with less-than, are not fun. They are the ones who never want to try the cake you made, or stay for one more drink, or buy the ridiculously overpriced meal, or share fries at dawn after a night out. People might fantasize about having more self-control in their own lives, but that's not the person they want to be, or be friends with. Control is the pilferer of joy, the embezzler of freedom.

Last fall I visited Kirsten over Thanksgiving. It was a mostly great weekend. The weather was crisp and sunny, we went for boozy pedicures and took the kids to the science museum, and jewel-toned leafy parks, and saw a movie about Superpets (it's a thing, okay? Those dogs are freaking heroes). We walked around her new neighborhood and had creative cocktails and cozy glasses of wine. And we went for a fancy dinner double date.

And this past weekend it was Thanksgiving again. And I thought about that weekend. And I texted Kirsten to say that I miss her. And she mentioned how much fun it had been and that she wished that we were back at that beautiful restaurant having that beautiful dinner. That horrible, awful dinner where I couldn't be present because I was so worried about what to order. And how I'd eat what I'd ordered. And if anyone had noticed that I hadn't eaten what I ordered. Or if anyone would notice when I went to cry in the bathroom because I was so frustrated and sad that despite all the practice, I was still so afraid of so many things. I don't remember what we talked about, but the discomfort is a sense memory. If I think about it long enough, I get shame goose bumps* (*patent pending).

There are movies where I can't recall the main characters' names, but I can remember my stomach rumbling in the dark theater. Nights out with big happy groups where I didn't hear a word anyone said until the food had been cleared away. Drink nights where everyone else had homemade sangria and signature cocktails, and I stuck to wine. A collage of control and deprivation.

I wonder what it would have been like to have eaten the delicious things and drank the drinks (this sounds wrong, maybe if all the calorie counts were taking up less brain space I'd have more room for grammar). Could I have enjoyed those things without worrying about how they might affect my body?

The other night I went for a midnight swim in my small backyard pool with Kevin and Neil. It was dark; we only had the pool lights on. And they are gay men (the actual gayest when it comes to not noticing women's bodies—or women in general—Neil still can't tell any of my female friends apart), and they are two of the people I love the most. Yet I was so self-conscious in my bathing suit that it was distracting. And since then I have fantasized about returning to old disordered habits, so I don't have to feel that way again.

I found myself wondering if more freedom around food and movement means debilitating self-consciousness every time I have to wear a bathing suit/yoga clothes/a fitted shirt for the rest of my life. And if so, if it's actually worth it.

The next morning, I thought about the cardio machines in my home gym and how easy it would be to use them and feel better and then get on with my day with less guilt, and stress, and sadness. How if I were to keep it up, I might start to feel better about my body.

But how futile that would be. Because I would be reinforcing the notion that I am no more than a body. It's insulting to myself, and to my friends who don't like me more, or less, based on how I look in a bathing suit.

I hated that my bigger body (or how I felt about my body) took away from what was otherwise a wonderful night. Though acting like my body is the most important thing about me has taken away from hundreds of wonderful nights. The problem isn't with my body.

The problem was never with my body.

CHAPTER 40

Everyone has problems that are hard and real. Though sometimes I fantasize about having someone else's. Lately I've been thinking that maybe I'd like recovery from alcoholism better.

Before you say it, I understand that this is ridiculous. I don't know what it's like to recover from anyone else's thing. Just as I bet that every alcoholic among the tens of people reading this book looks at my problem and doesn't get why it's so hard to eat a damn sandwich. The grass is always greener on the other side of the addiction center.

The thing that I find enviable is that alcoholics have a more clear-cut recovery manual. STOP DRINKING THE THING. My manual states that I must consume more and more of my thing to stay alive, and the method options for doing so are completely confusing (intuitive eating? eating to satiety? meal plans?) and often overwhelming. I don't get to fix my eating disorder by cutting out the thing that's causing me all of the stress, I have to have *more* of it, almost immediately after I wake up. And then again, and again, and again and again.

Also, to my mind, people understand alcoholism. They get that it's physiological. No one thinks that alcoholics are vapid and vain and deluded (unless they are, but that's not because of the alcoholism).

There are obviously many fun variations on this game—the hierarchy of addictions I'd maybe rather be recovering from:

Alcohol: Yes

Heroin: No

Weed: Yes

Sex: Maybe?

Gambling: No

Plastic surgery: Absolutely not.

Oprah keeps a gratitude journal, and I keep a running list of mental illnesses I might prefer. We are both very, very evolved.

This game is obviously asinine. All of us have to do the thing that we find the hardest to get better. That's simply how recovery works. If I felt the urge to drink whenever I feel stressed or anxious, that would feel as strong and unrelenting as the urge to move or restrict. I get it. Addiction is a harsh and exhausting fight, in every form. Everyone's hard thing can seem easy to people who have different hard things.

But here's what we all have: we are more empathetic. We are less judgmental. I understand what it's like to feel the constant magnetic pull of the worst thing for you. This struggle has helped me see and connect with other people in a way that I wouldn't have been able to, but for trying to recover from my own thing.

I appreciate knowing that we are all woven from the same cloth, and that we are all fighting similar battles. Feeling less alone is always a nice perk.

CHAPTER 41

There was a girl in the children's hospital who wanted to get better. She was older than me, and I knew her name because she was the one regular with whom I'd never overlapped. She was smart and quiet with huge eyes and a genuine smile. Her straight chin-length hair was light red, and her skin was freckled and tinted yellow-orange from eating too many vegetables rich in beta carotene, and not much else. (I recognized this in her immediately, having gone through more than one yellowish phase myself. We were clearly years ahead of the self-tanning industry.)

When we met, she was in her room taping inspirational sayings and articles disparaging fashion media on her wall. I asked her why (I tended toward classier wall coverings in the form of posters of kittens and James Dean), to which she simply said, "We're really sick, and I want to get better." I didn't know what to make of it. I'd never heard any patient admit that they were sick, let alone suggest that I was too. I really thought that we all shared the same goals: stay out of the hospital, but also, stay thin. I wish that I'd asked her some questions, or that we'd had a conversation about this. I was gobsmacked, and we didn't. I was discharged before she was, and I never saw her again. In my fantasy, she did get well.

Unlike teenagers today who have access to (or are the creators behind) countless recovery accounts on Instagram, YouTube, and TikTok, the only people I knew who were like me were girls I'd met in the hospital. So I didn't know anyone who had recovered. Or anyone who was trying to recover. Or that recovery was a thing.

When I started undergrad, I considered anorexia a thing of my past, like glittery eye shadow and aerosol hairspray. I even wrote a piece for a third-year magazine writing assignment that I later sold to a women's magazine about the behavior modification protocols that were so widely used at the time to treat anorexia in children's hospitals, and how damaging they were, implying that it was a G-damned miracle that I'd managed to recover despite it. I also met a friend at the gym who had gone through the same treatment (*I know!* Shocking that we met at the gym and not Chick-fil-A) whom I'd interviewed for my article and secretly deemed "not-really-better." Clearly, the only thing I was better at than endless hours of cardio was living in a state of total denial.

I'd ended that magazine piece with a story about a sweet girl I'd been friends with who had been in and out of the hospital with me. She died of a heart attack at age nineteen. And I wasn't dead. So obviously, I was well.

Thinking back to how I could have thought I was well when I was still so very ill, is sort of like hearing about all the stuff you did when you were drunk. It comes back in bits and pieces (*oh yeah!* That's why my elbow hurts and there's a rip in my shirt!). My university friends all thought I was anorexic because all I ate was salad and freezies, and I thought that I was better because I ate! Salad *and* freezies! I cringe at the memories of the very few times I told people about the eating disorder that I *used to* have (generally when concerned friends asked if I was okay). Though I told almost no one. It was my most disgraceful secret.

I moved back to my hometown after law school and worried a lot about bumping into someone who might know about my past, who might tell someone who didn't. This worry was actualized when a guy I'd been dating for a couple of months found out third-hand from his young niece, who'd heard it from her singing teacher. I'd told his niece that I'd had the same teacher as a teenager, and the teacher told her when she mentioned my name. He was upset that I'd never said anything, and he obviously knew I was lying when I said food wasn't a problem for me anymore. The thing is I didn't know that it *wasn't* not a problem for me anymore. I still remember telling him that it was like something that had happened to another person and that I couldn't even relate to the feelings I used to have. I also remember the look he exchanged with his sister when I couldn't eat any of the food she prepared for the Friday night dinner at her house.

I didn't stay with men who were onto my weird eating problems or my crazy exercise schedule. And I got better at making up excuses that sounded more and more believable, having had over a decade to workshop them. Also, the fact that I didn't really understand the magnitude of my problem (I knew I didn't want to gain weight, but didn't know I had a mental illness) was also helpful in terms of keeping it real.

When I told my now-husband a year after we'd started dating, and a few months before we moved into our first house, I framed it as a problem I'd had in the past. And he believed me. I also knew that he didn't understand and that he accepted my shame as a normal consequence of having had such a shameful secret. We didn't talk about it again for about ten years.

We didn't ever go to hotels that didn't have a gym, or restaurants whose menus I hadn't pre-screened. Food from my plate at banquets and weddings and conferences and dinners out and people's homes would end up on his plate quickly and inconspicuously. He would faithfully eat my dinners, and recite my many food intolerances to friends, family, and waiters. He was my anorexia beard without ever knowing it.

This isn't all that different from my mother, who still leaves my salad undressed and has special food set aside for me on the rare occasion that we go over for a meal. I used to think she believed I recovered years ago, but I'm not sure any more. She might be more like my high school friends, who, having seen me at my worst, presume that not-really-well is as well as I'm going to get.

And I understand that, mostly. Why the people in my life who are the closest to me presumed that food would forever be an issue but never asked if I was okay. I mean if I was in denial, why couldn't the rest of them be in denial too?

CHAPTER 42

Despite always knowing I wanted to be a mother, I had always feared I wouldn't be able to have children. I had never had a natural period, and I was pretty sure my insides were broken.

I mentioned this to my family doctor after my now-husband and I got engaged, and she referred us to a local fertility center. A few months later, I found myself explaining my medical history and spreading my legs for an orthodox Jew a few years younger than my father. He recommended a drug that would hopefully make me ovulate and told me to start on it right away, as it often takes a while to work. It didn't occur to anyone to ask me about my eating habits or question my weight, which wasn't dangerously low, but low enough that I wasn't getting a period. I took the magic pills and got pregnant that first month (all those months of boxer briefs and not letting my husband put his laptop within a three-mile radius of his lap paid off). I was eleven weeks pregnant at our wedding.

Pregnancy was terrifying and magical. I stopped working in order to spend hours Googling what fruit my baby most resembled and what to do to keep him safe. To be clear, I was still going into work every day, I was just spending most of my time on pregnancy websites. My OB weighed me at my monthly appointments, but I quickly learned that it was to make sure I wasn't gaining too *much* weight. I started showing around the end of my fifth month and got a lot of compliments for the fact that the only part of me that looked pregnant was the bump (and my massive-for-me breasts). For the first time in my life, I loved how I looked in fitted shirts (and V-necks!).

The baby was small, but as long as he kept growing, the doctor wasn't concerned. I'd sometimes worry I wasn't eating enough, but the doctor would always reassure me his small size wasn't my fault ("you don't get a rat from a mouse!"). I'd also read stories about people in third-world countries and in wartime who gave birth to healthy babies, and I took great comfort in the fact my baby would take whatever he needed from my body (calcium? All yours! Iron? Have some of mine!).

It was a strange dichotomy. On the one hand, I was so careful about all the things I had to avoid—I accidentally ate fresh fennel in a salad once and called my OB in a panic. I read the ingredients in herbal tea, wouldn't go near anyone who was eating sushi (or contemplating eating sushi), gave up coffee, and didn't even have a sip of wine at my own wedding. But when it came to eating all the dietary fat I needed, or even eating every time I was hungry, well, those things felt less important than holding my breath every time I saw someone smoking from my car window.

I wasn't starving myself. I was eating in a way that was me-normal plus 200 extra calories, which is what the internet said I needed to grow an extra human. And I was exercising. Not excessively, but more than most pregnant people.

Somewhere around week 32 the baby started showing quite small for dates. His heart rate, muscle tone, movement, breathing, and the amount of amniotic fluid around him were all fine—he was even seen sucking his fingers, which got him ultrasound bonus points (a habit that his orthodontist found less impressive eleven years later), but he wasn't growing as quickly as expected. I had a niggle it was because of me—that I needed to be moving less and eating more. Then the voice in my head reminded me I was eating more than people in Sudan, who give birth to healthy babies *all. the. time.*

After a few weeks of slower-than-expected growth, my OB sent me and my husband to see a doctor who specialized in high-risk pregnancies. It was the end of my 35th week. She looked at the results of his biophysical profile (he scored six out of five! Our kid was an actual genius!) and said he was probably fine and that if we chose to induce, he might have latching problems, and that his lungs might not be fully developed right away and that he'd be more work for us, but ultimately fine. I asked what would happen if we chose not to induce and let him keep cooking, at least until a date when we could know for sure he had fully formed lungs. And she said he'd likely be fine but that he might die; she wasn't totally sure.

It was a Friday evening. We spent the entire weekend buying baby things (a Jewish superstition had prevented me from doing so earlier in my pregnancy). Monday I went to put my Y membership on hold, hand in my work pass, and to find someone to take care of my office plant (I chose well, it's still alive). Tuesday morning, I did a cardio workout in my home gym and waited for the call from the hospital.

It took our son two days to come out. And while two days of contractions made me feel less guilty about not being in the gym (talk about an ab workout!), I was flooded with guilt as I felt my sweet boy moving around inside me. I knew he deserved his last four weeks in the womb and my disgusting selfishness had taken that from him.

He was born on the Thursday afternoon, with fully formed lungs and the sweetest, most beautiful little face I'd ever seen (I know some people say that about their not-cute babies, but my kid was objectively gorgeous. You can ask my husband or my mother). He was 4 pounds, 13 ounces, tiny, but perfectly proportioned.

The week after he was born was the longest I'd ever gone without a workout. Breastfeeding burns as many calories as cardio, and I was feeding him every three hours around the clock, so I rationalized the break. I was back in my old jeans before his two-week check-up.

In quiet moments I would search things like "effect of low-fat diet on birth weight" or "impact of exercise in pregnancy on birth weight" online. I couldn't shake the feeling that I'd caused my baby's smallness and early eviction from my womb. In addition to the fact my husband was a small baby, I have since learned there is a correlation between the drug I took to ovulate and low-birth-weight babies, but in my heart of hearts, I still blame myself and am so grateful that my son—and his sisters—were okay.

CHAPTER 43

Calorie Counting is Stupid, Not an Ode

By: Me

> Calorie counting is stupid
> Calorie counting is dumb
> There used to be a time
> When I was afraid of the calories in a stick of sugarless gum.
>
> It made me afraid to try anything new
> Or eat at anyone's house
> You could offer me your homemade soup
> But I'd rather have French kissed a mouse.
>
> Calories, measurements, numbers
> Monopolize the thoughts in my head
> They pop up and demand to be re-added
> When I am talking, or writing, or reading to my kids before bed.
>
> They don't care if I'm hungry or full
> Or if making them fit causes something to taste really bad
> And until very recently they prevented me from understanding
> That dry salad is actually quite sad.

The numbers on packages are not even accurate
There is a huge margin of error
And I know that I am progressing
Because this fact no longer causes me terror.

Calories don't account for the fact
That food is broken down in different ways
There are variances among the exact same foods
When you eat them on different days.

People break down food at different metabolic rates
And have different bacteria in their guts
There are even differences among the way we absorb
Whole or chopped up nuts.

Splenda, Stevia, Malitol
Koji noodles, cauliflower rice
Sugarless fat-free ice cream
None of you taste nice.

I'd like for these numbers to go away
And for my body to take over from here
To tell me what it likes and wants
And to be able to listen without fear.

I don't know why I worry so much
About making choices on my own
Why what I put in my mouth
Is dictated by numbers on my phone.

I can pick out my own food
Based on what I crave
I feel like my body knows better
than these numbers that keep me enslaved.

So Mr. Atwater, scientist
From two hundred years ago
Take your calorie discovery and shove it
It's stuff I wish I didn't know.

CHAPTER 44

Ambivalence in recovery is something people who aren't in it just don't get. Why not stop exercising and eat all the cake if that's the cure? What could be easier than eating and sitting around? Just do it, get it over with, and you will feel better!

The thing is, it's not that easy. Because while these are things many people find pleasurable, they are the scariest things for me to do.

Are you arachnophobic? If yes, I can help! I'm not at all afraid of spiders (they are surprisingly low-calorie). All you have to do is lie around in a bed of spiders every day—but you can watch TV and stuff while you are lying with the spiders, you know, as a distraction for when you feel them crawling all over your arms and legs and face.

Maybe when you aren't lying with the spiders, you will still feel them, or be thinking about your next lie-in, but don't worry! The more accustomed you are to spiders crawling on you, the faster you will stop caring about them. And then, when lying with ten spiders feels almost okay, we will bump you up to fifty. That's the way to do it. Don't be anxious!

And don't worry about getting bitten. Sure, they will probably bite you quite a lot, and you might have to get some new baggier pants to accommodate all the bites, but you will get used to them! Yes, some people consider spider bites unattractive, but everyone knows it's what's inside that counts. You can always get some big sweaters and sweatpants to hide all of the bites. Really, no one else even cares what you look like, and if they do, they aren't worth your time.

Oh, and sorry. This will eventually work, but we have no specific timeline. Because you've been afraid of spiders for so long, it's possible that you'll need to sleep with spiders every night for three years before the fear completely goes away. And in the meantime, there are people who are going to expect the worst and tell you that you will always be a little afraid of them. They will tell you that for some people arachnophobia is a life-long struggle, or not a big deal if it prevents you from getting unattractive spider bites, and you will have to ignore those people and climb into your bed of spiders.

For me, it's the messiness of recovery that mucks everything up. How long is it all going to take? How much weight will I gain? How many more times do I have to eat that thing before it stops feeling scary? Why can't there be a manual? I understand that lots of things don't come with manuals. I have three children and zero idea what I'm doing most of the time (because no manual), but I would really appreciate a guarantee that if you do all the things in a certain order for a predetermined amount of time, you will be done.

And yes, I *know* life generally doesn't work like that. In fact, we have no control over most things [*insert terrible and unpredictable tragedy here*]. But there is still a blueprint that works the majority of the time for the majority of people in mostly the same way.

When you go to school you can ask other people who did the same program what to expect, and that's pretty much what you can expect. Study for tests. Get your assignments done on time. Don't show up to class hammered. Don't plagiarize. Don't go to medical school if you are afraid of blood, or law school if you are afraid of books, or circus school if you afraid of clowns. Do those things, and you will most likely succeed in the exact same manner as the people who came before you. And that gives us comfort, even though we all know deep down that everything can go off the rails at any time.

In eating disorder recovery, we have a tendency to look for people who recovered from illnesses that looked just like ours as proof that we too can succeed. And while this can feel comforting, it can also be debilitating. We are all so different. Some people don't have fear foods, or exercise addictions, or body dysmorphia. Some people have experienced terrible trauma, and some haven't been ill for very long and have clear memories of being happy and healthy. Some people recover quickly by going all-in and never looking back, and some of us are too afraid to jump, and take smaller, more gradual steps.

I don't know anyone with a history exactly like mine, let alone someone with a history exactly like mine who has fully recovered. And the only person I know whose history is more like mine than anyone else's has relapsed twice in the time I've known her and thinks that full recovery is a myth, like unicorns, and dust mites. But that has absolutely nothing to do with me, or my recovery.

Recovery (I guess like life) boils down to faith. Faith that it will work out. Faith that eating the greasy Thai food that made you cry, and kept you up last night, is rewiring the neural pathways in your brain. Faith that resting when you want to go for a walk (or a run) will change your relationship with your body and movement for the better. Faith that as your body grows, your life will too. And that the eating disorder noise that is so much louder when you are trying to recover than it is when you aren't, will soon reach a crescendo and then fall to a level where it's hardly discernible. And that you will be free.

Faith can be impossibly hard to find some days, but it's the only way out. Having faith is not a guarantee of success (you also have to do the hard things), but not having enough faith probably guarantees failure.

But for the record, I'd choose to lie in a bed of spiders over eating a plate of Thai food in a hot minute.

CHAPTER 45

Everyone with an eating disorder lies. Even if you're someone who isn't a great liar in life, (maybe you give too much detail or can't make eye contact or can't keep your story straight), your eating disorder comes with the gift of Oscar-quality acting abilities when it comes to lying about what you've eaten, where you've eaten, whether you've eaten, whether you've exercised and how much exercise you've done. Even if you're someone who thinks that lying is wrong, you will be able to distance yourself from ED lies in a way that is almost magical.

If there were awards for things like "Best Lie About Whether You Ate Before You Got Here" or "Most Convincing Story About Why You Can't Eat Salad Dressing," I don't know how they would narrow it down. Every single one of us would deserve a trophy for our ability to look our friends/partners/spouses/parents/children in the eye and say, "Oh, no thank you. I just ate."

For me, the lying started in grade seven, when I started bringing two cans of club soda and three plain rice cakes to school for lunch every day (eventually cutting out the rice cakes). Charged with making my own lunch and my siblings' lunches, I would pack sandwiches and snacks for my brother and sister and then quickly slip my own low-cal-low-sugar-low-fat-low-protein-high-air lunch into my school bag while no one was looking.

By grade eight, I was lying about what I'd eaten and diet pills (mainly to the pharmacists selling them to me, and once to a friend who saw them inside my bag). By grade nine, I was lying about what I'd eaten, a very brief foray into laxative abuse (zero stars. Do not recommend), and water-loading. I lied about water-loading for four years straight, including within hours of being caught water-loading. The fact that I could get caught and still get away with lying about it later the same day was a testament to my ED-lying superpower.

I lied about how thin I was by hiding my protruding bones beneath layers of clothing, I lied about how scared I was by pretending I couldn't feel my heart beating in my chest. I lied about body checking and about not being hungry and about getting better when I wasn't.

When I was in grade eleven, I also started lying about smoking—I told my parents that I'd stopped. Occasionally, they'd ask if I was sure that I'd stopped, and I'd assure them that I had and the reason I sometimes smelled of smoke was because I'd been around smokers. And then one day my dad pulled out every lighter and pack of cigarettes I'd thought I misplaced over the past three months. Caught. I couldn't string three words together, let alone articulate an excuse or explanation. Proof that the ED-lying superpower only translates to ED things.

Up until recently, I would arrive two hours late to your birthday party if it was a sit-down dinner—no matter how much I liked you—so I could avoid the meal. I would meet you somewhere and tell you I'd gotten a lift or that I'd walked because I had to run an errand on the way. I would tell you that I had tried it, and it was *delicious*. I would tell you I'd have loved to have some, but I was allergic. At the day program, I lied about my weight and how much I was eating and moving on the weekends. I lied to my friends about eating before I got here, and there, and everywhere.

When it comes to the ED these days, there are people I never lie to (a couple of my closest friends), and people I practically never lie to (my coach), and people I very rarely lie to (the rest of my closest friends). But that's new for me. I have benefited over and over and over in ways that are almost unquantifiable from the simple act of being honest with the people around me, and yet my first instinct is still to lie.

Though the most curious lies are the ones we tell ourselves.

I tell myself I want to recover then use artificial sweetener in my tea. I tell myself I'm taking a break from exercise then take the longest route possible to the store. I tell everyone who will listen that diet culture is bullshit and contributes to the oppression of women and a waste of our precious time, and then waste time and brain space and energy tallying calories up in my head and *hating* myself for the way I look in my jeans.

I lie to myself more than I lie to anyone around me. I am still the worst kind of lying liar.

Though the eating disorder also lies to me. It tells me my life was better when I was smaller. It tells me my only value is in the way I look and that I don't deserve to rest or to be fully nourished. It tells me that I will never fully recover, so what's the point. It tells me that this is as good as it's going to get and that I need to stop before my weight gets even more out of control, and I can never go back.

And you'd think a skilled liar such as myself would be better at recognizing lies. But I'm not.

There are days I believe all of it.

Even as I write this, I can pick out the parts I'm not supposed to believe—the parts that the people I love and trust tell me are lies—but today, they feel like gospel.

CHAPTER 46

I have a lot of trouble eating things I don't like (and as discussed, things that are too high-calorie, too-hard-to count, too-unnecessary, or when I'm not hungry). Things I don't like is a notable one though because it doesn't apply across the board; there are weird rules. (*What? Weird food rules? No!*)

Taking all other variables out of the equation—let's say I'm hungry, and the food is relatively countable, and it's a meal (so presumably necessary), I still have a very hard time eating anything I deem slightly unsavory. Unless it's low enough in calories for the taste to be irrelevant.

Picture a chart where the vertical axis applies to how much I like something and the horizontal axis applies to caloric density. And let's call the diagonal the "chocolate diagonal" (it's calorie-dense and something I like). Anything that falls on or below the chocolate diagonal passes the test as something I can eat and anything above feels impossibly hard.

For example, overcooked mushy cauliflower would fall below the chocolate diagonal if it were unbuttered (don't like it very much, but low calorie). However, if the same cauliflower were buttered and salted, that would increase the palatability on the taste axis, but the extra calories would put it over the chocolate diagonal.

As the calories get higher, so does the amount I have to like it. I won't eat a vanilla cupcake, but I might eat a chocolate one.

Unless it's iced, which puts it too high on the calorie axis, given that I've never been a big fan of icing (even as a kid).

So obviously the best foods for me are things like apples (I really like them, and they aren't high in calories). Unless the apple is bruised or too mushy or too sweet or too sour. So basically, as long as it's the perfect apple, I'm in.

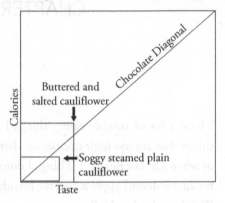

This has shaped my tastes. It explains why I contentedly ate dry salad for so many years and why I'm still happiest eating a package of frozen tofu and steamed broccoli for dinner (mostly-palatable, not-scary and bonus: microwavable—my favorite kind of cooking).

In order for a lower volume, higher-calorie food to be worth it, it has to taste amazing (is this cookie ≥ four heads of broccoli? The broccoli will fill me up, the cookie will not. Therefore, the cookie is purely for pleasure. Do I even deserve to derive pleasure from food?). My brain has been hardwired to see higher-calorie foods as danger. With that said, over the course of this recovery effort, I've gotten better at eating higher-calorie things simply because I like them. And once I know I like something, I don't want to deviate from it. Why waste calories on the unknown if I can eat something I know I like?

There is a flood of guilt and noise when I eat something higher calorie that I don't like. Though this doesn't apply strictly to high-calorie foods—I have trouble finishing an apple that doesn't feel "worth it" (but not dried out cucumber slices that have been to school and back, sitting in a lunch bag all day, and likely touched by dirty child-fingers).

The feeling that all calories above a certain threshold—somewhere between cucumber slices and apple—have to be worth it likely stems from the fact that I spent so many years trying to make sure I was eating the lowest number of calories possible. Taste was a mostly irrelevant consideration.

Some of it is the messaging I grew up with. My mother is known to leave things on her plate that she deems "not worth the calories," and when I was a chubby ten-year-old, that was the litmus test she promoted with the conviction of a weight-loss professional (not simply someone in a work-from-home volunteer position). And some of it is pure anorexic scarcity mindset. Every food in my daily caloric quota has to be perfect, and worthy.

This is obviously a problem. Not only is it grossly entitled, but it's also constraining. It means that there are a lot of things I can't eat. Not everyone is a great cook, myself included. And it would feel weird to have to provide hosts with a copy of the graph and a brief explanation of how it works anytime I'm invited somewhere for dinner and they ask about dietary restrictions (and I feel like most restaurants wouldn't take it very seriously). I also don't generally like the taste of things that I'm unfamiliar with, or I find scary, which therefore eliminates a lot of things that might pass the test with some practice.

What's the solution? Reminding myself that only privileged asshats refuse to eat things because they don't like them? Telling myself that food is really just food and doesn't have to be a perfect taste experience every time? Forcing myself to eat things regardless of whether I like them or not? Yes.

It all feels so counterintuitive. I generally don't finish books I don't like, and never finish shows I don't like, and I mostly try to avoid hanging out with people I don't like. And—when surveyed—my (non-disordered) friends all said they don't eat things that they don't like. Though on reflection, that's different from not being *able* to eat things they don't like. If they are at someone's house, or very hungry, they will eat what's available to them. I also suspect that their list of unlikable things is much shorter than mine.

If I've learned anything in this process, it's that my intuition can't be trusted right now. My relationship with food and guilt is still too complicated for me to make good decisions. Until I learn how to detach myself from the guilt and judgment, I need to start eating things I don't like. Maybe I'll even end up liking some of them. I finished a book last week that I mostly couldn't stand, and the ending made it worth it.

CHAPTER 47

The summer before grade seven, a few months after I had started restricting and a few months before I'd develop full-blown anorexia, I told my boyfriend (my first) that I was worried I was fat.

And that sweet, skinny, gangly, metal-mouthed boy who smelled of baby powder and stepped on my toes approximately ten times per slow dance told me to put my ankles together and check if there was a gap between my thighs. If there was, I was not fat.

And so I did. And twelve-year-old me breathed a sigh of relief. Not. Fat.

Of course with time, as the illness progressed, a thigh gap wasn't enough. It was thumb and index finger looped around arms, and fingers on jutting hip bones, and fists beneath rib cage. But the thigh gap was always the first thing I checked. Religiously, twice a day, standing with my heels together, gaging my size and my worth by the size of that space.

Eventually, happily, gradually, as the illness loosened its grip, my arms filled out. There is no longer a cavernous gap between hip bone and hip, or ribs and abdomen. But my obsession with that space between my thighs has remained. And this week, for the first time, my thighs touched in the middle.

Panic.

I look at my young daughters' thighs, and I realize how ridiculous it would be to place any of their worth in the air in-between the beautiful legs that carry them around and allow them to jump and dance and stomp (extra-loud when I'm trying to sleep).

And then I think about my own legs and all they have been through. The times they have healed from fractures despite not getting enough rest or calories for repair. The times I have called them disgusting. The times they carried my pregnant body, and my sick starving one.

Today (and every day until I know it's true) I will remind myself that touching thighs are a sign of progress. That gap was clearly no more than a space for the eating disorder. I'm taking back that space, and my life.

Goodbye, thigh gap.

CHAPTER 48

November 3, 2020

<u>To Do, 3.0</u>

- Keep challenging fear foods
- Keep eating uncountable things
- Stop trying to count the uncountable things
- Stop walking so much
- Buy some new jeans
- Get rid of old jeans that no longer fit
- Stop berating yourself for the fact that some of your jeans no longer fit
- Stop fantasizing about taking a recovery break so your jeans can fit again
- Seriously, stop it
- Stop it
- Stop
- It

CHAPTER 49

I grew up with little pink packets of fake sugar in my parents' house. I am so accustomed to the taste of cyclamate that sugar initially tasted weird—not sweet enough, chemically enough, cloying enough.

I traveled with it (like a fancy camera, but lighter and less useful). There were always some at the bottom of my purse (like lipstick, but lighter and less useful) and in coat pockets (like a wallet, but lighter and less useful). I bought it in bulk and knew which Starbucks carried the kind I like (pink, never blue or yellow).

I used it in oatmeal. In smoothies. On tart fruit. In lattes and in lemonade. In hot tea and iced tea. In plain yogurt. And on my icy driveway to stop my kids from slipping (okay, not that one). Pink packet after pink packet. Shake shake shake, rip, pour. Over and over. All day long.

And then, I stopped using it in food (because I was ordered to. Apparently zero-calorie powdered chemicals are not aligned with my recovery goals).

I learned to like the taste of maple syrup in yogurt, brown sugar in oatmeal, white sugar in milky coffee drinks. Though I kept using it in tea. Tea didn't count (see subparagraph 2(1)(b)(iii) of the *Hypocrisy and Rationalization Act*).

I drink a lot of tea in the winter, and I thought about my teeth bathing in all that sugar water and the fact that tea doesn't provide any nutritional value whatsoever. So why would it need calories? Calories in tea feel unnecessary.

But it's not about my teeth. I've never had a cavity and suspect this won't be the thing to put me over the edge. It's about needing to micromanage everything that goes into my mouth.

I can't try to avoid "unnecessary" calories while recovering from an illness that will try to convince me every calorie is an unnecessary calorie. It's no different from my commitment to butter toast and to use salad dressing and to buy full-fat cheese. If I continue to pander to the disorder, where will it end? It won't. I will never have the freedom to eat ice cream with my kids on a lazy afternoon, or hot cookies right out of the oven, or a piece of wedding cake, if I don't believe that all calories are fine, that all food is safe.

It's tough though. As a teenager I remember not being able to wrap my head around the idea that anyone would buy a soft drink that wasn't diet, and I still have to work really hard to add fat to recipes (why yes, my famous vinegar and vinegar salad dressing *is* a little on the tart side). I think that it's going to take a lot of effort and practice before it feels totally normal.

I know I have to do it though, because on reflection, what could be more necessary than the lesson that I can drink sugared tea and be just fine?

CHAPTER 50

I've been doing cardio again.

It's only been two days, and I'm deciding whether I want to keep going or treat it like it was a slip.

I've been pretty confident in my divorce from this piece of equipment since giving it up last spring, but giving it up hasn't fixed me. It's made me feel worse about my body and more anxious about walking enough (which for anyone keeping track is far more time-consuming than a bit of cardio in the mornings). It's made me feel different and broken compared to people who can exercise, grab themselves a few endorphins, and move on with their day.

With that said, I didn't get on the elliptical machine yesterday because I wanted to celebrate my newfound body confidence with a dose of endorphins. I got on because I felt fat. And lazy. And in my heart of hearts, I want to get back to a weight where I don't feel these things.

Which is such a cliché; it's embarrassing. Woman with eating disorder starts exercising because she's unhappy in her body and thinks that will make her feel happy. I'm basically a parody of myself.

But what if exercise gave me the confidence I need to keep going in recovery?

Just because I hopped on a cardio machine doesn't mean I'm going to start restricting or skipping meals or weighing food. It just means that I want to be a normal person who's able to exercise if I want to.

I don't want to tell anyone about this because it will seem like a regression, but I don't think that's right. Because for regression to happen, there would have to have been real progress, and it felt too easy to go back.

So maybe I need to change my expectations.

I have been in recovery for years now. Actual years. And I still don't feel ready to gain more weight in exchange for freedom. I'm starting to really believe that it's too late for me. My self-worth and my weight will forever be interconnected.

I would like to be an example of peaceful body acceptance for my children, but I've lost faith in the idea that being this distracted and unhappy will lead to better things for any of us.

If a piece of plastic and metal (etcetera, I'm not handy, I don't know how things are made) will make me feel less awful about my body and less distracted around my kids, and less strange and deprived around people who talk about exercise, why not?

There's obviously a risk that letting this one sneaky behavior back in will lead me back into a spiral of restriction, like a smoker who can't have a drink without a cigarette. I'll have to be really mindful of that.

I'll give it a week and see how it feels. I'm tired of living in a *Fear Factor* rerun, hoping that each day will be the one that might feel okay.

CHAPTER 51

I had a friend in high school who met all her boyfriends, even one whom she would eventually marry and later divorce, at McDonalds. She had a part-time job there and dated her way through every one of the guys, eventually working her way up to a boyfriend in middle management. I don't think that it was because she really loved the smell of grease on a man, but rather that's where she spent most of her free time. Similarly, through all of undergrad and law school, I met most of my boyfriends at the gym.

I'm not going to lie; this was a pretty impressive feat on my part. Because unlike some girls who went to the gym looking fresh and pretty, with a splash of lipstick or perfume, I was a sweaty, sweaty, sweaty mess. Though I also knew enough to shower, dry my hair, and come back in to chat for a minute on the way out if I really had my eye on someone.

There was Dan (school gym), an exceptionally cute university gym employee and third-year business student I worked really hard to get to like me, only to discover on our first and only date that he was a terrible conversationalist when it came to all things not exercise-related (but if you wanted to discuss the merits of doing chest on your arm day versus on your back day, he was your guy). There was Keith (YMCA), a thirty-three-year-old trader who was still in love with his ex who had moved back to Japan the previous summer; there was Matt (school gym), a very handsome, funny not-quite-recovering alcoholic who was also still in love with his ex (who'd dumped him because of his drinking); there was Jon (private gym), a genuinely nice, attractive older guy, who I could have been nicer to; and finally Rick (YMCA), my lying, screwed up, often sweet, gym rat, personal-trainer boyfriend of four years.

The nice thing about meeting someone at the gym was that we would be able to see each other. I thought I wanted a boyfriend, because the idea of companionship seemed kind of nice, but I didn't really have time for a boyfriend, given my very important relationship with the elliptical machine/Stairmaster/stationary bike. So even the gym boyfriends were people I kept at a distance. Until Rick.

Rick was funny and handsome and damaged in ways different from the ways that I was damaged. And he understood the way I ate. He trained people for bodybuilding competitions and had trained for one himself—once you go two weeks only eating cod for breakfast, lunch, and dinner, you don't really care if your girlfriend refuses to eat dietary fat and asks the movie theater employee to confirm multiple times that her Coke is diet before she'll drink it. The fact that he noticed how I ate and exercised but never questioned it made me feel closer to him than anyone else. That he knew how many calories were in a bagel, and to make my omelettes using egg whites only and *no. oil. whatsoever.* was a relief. The fact that I didn't have to keep that part of myself a secret around him was exhilarating. And he always smelled great.

He also didn't try to change or fix me. When I wanted to spend three hours at the gym on a Saturday morning, he was okay with that. When I needed to wear a heart-rate monitor when we went hiking, that was okay too. He understood why I needed my body to stay a certain way, because his did as well. And he was really funny. And I was attracted to him and his fitness-magazine body.

But our relationship wasn't good. He lied to everyone, including me, about everything. He had long bouts of depression, when he wouldn't answer my calls when I was at school 400 miles away. The first year and a half we were together, he had another girlfriend (want to cheat on someone? Find an exercise addict in her last year of law school. It will take her forever to notice). The weird thing is that I'm pretty certain that he did love me. And I loved him. But we were both so broken. I was being eaten alive by my exercise addiction, and on reflection, I don't think either of us really felt like we deserved to be loved.

We eventually broke up because I caught him in one too many lies. By then we had been together for about four years, and I was nearing thirty. I was a lawyer starting my career and knew that if I didn't want to marry this guy, we had to break up. And I didn't want to marry him. We fought all the time, and he lied about everything from why he was late (late people: why can't you guys ever just say, "sorry I'm late, I left late?"), to what he was doing, to who he was spending his time with. He lied about little things and big things. For obvious reasons and for no reason at all.

Even though I knew it was the right thing to do, it was a heart-wrenching breakup. I cried a lot because I missed him, and because I worried no one would ever accept me and my weird baggage again.

He got engaged within a few months of our breakup and got married the following spring, and to my surprise my siblings and my brother-in-law attended his wedding to a woman I suspected he'd started dating in the last couple of months we were together. I was hurt and confused, not so much by the wedding—I knew he desperately wanted to be married, a point of contention between us—but by my family's attendance. Had they really kept in touch with him in secret for all those months? My brother had spent endless hours listening to me cry about how much I missed him and agonizing over whether I'd made the right choice. How could they still be in touch?

It all came out a few weeks later. My brother and ex-boyfriend and brother-in-law had started a business together. They had been plotting in secret the entire time. My whole family knew, including my parents. They were all investors. They had kept it a secret from me, allegedly to protect me.

Oh, and in case you are wondering what kind of business it is, it's a weight-loss company.

The day I broke up with Rick, he had lied about where he was. I'd gotten off work early, and it was a beautiful late spring day. I was hoping to go sit on a patio somewhere and couldn't get hold of him. My mom called to say hi, and when I mentioned that Rick was missing, she casually told me he was golfing with my brother and brother-in-law. He hadn't told me because he knew my relationship with my brother-in-law was strained. When he called me back and lied about being with a client all afternoon, I broke up with him on the spot, over the phone, from my grey concrete apartment balcony, at 4 p.m. on a sunny Friday. It wasn't only the lie, but how blatant it was, like he wanted to get caught. Or didn't care if he was caught. I was done.

Many months later, I found out they were discussing their plan to start a full-service weight-loss company. Rick was to oversee personal training, my brother-in-law, a GP with a fresh bariatrician designation, was to be in charge of patient care, and my brother, a CFA with a degree in international business, was to handle the business side of things. My sister, a social worker, and my sister-in-law, a clinical psychologist would later come on board as well.

Having a family in the weight-loss business means that there is a lot of dinner-table diet talk. My brother-in-law (now-author of a best-selling diet book and a popular health and wellness blog) has been known to utter phrases like "there are two ways to spell waste" at the dinner table (*waist*. Get it?). He is revered by my parents (at one point I had to tell my mom to stop quoting him to me).

They aren't monsters. They truly believe obesity is a disease, and that they are helping people. If you are someone who works in the diet industry, or someone who buys into the diet industry, it's hard not to believe those things. Similarly, if you are someone trying to get over disordered eating, or diet culture, or a few decades of anorexia, or if you are someone who cares about ending unfair, hurtful, and damaging discrimination based on weight, this is the exact kind of thinking you need to unlearn.

Dr. Lindo Bacon, in their groundbreaking book *Health at Every Size: The Surprising Truth About Your Weight*, popularized the crazy, off-the-wall idea that people come in all shapes and sizes (what?!) and that you can't tell how healthy or unhealthy someone is by looking at their body. *Health at Every Size* (or *HAES*) recognizes that some people are meant to be fat, just as some people are meant to be thin, or tall, or short. If you have to restrict food to be in a thin body, you are not healthy. If you have to exercise obsessively to be in a thin body, you are not healthy.

It's been proven again and again, study after study, that people in thinner bodies don't live longer than people in fatter bodies. When you take into account factors such as socioeconomic status, fitness, activity, and nutrient intake, so-called "overweight" people do not have lower life expectancies than their thinner counterparts. That is, except as far as the serious medical concerns of people in bigger bodies who go to the doctor are routinely ignored. Swollen thyroid? Lose weight. Stomach pain? Lose weight. Sore ankle? Lose some weight. Lump in your breast? Lose weight. Depression? Have you tried losing weight? If you are fat, that's often all your doctor can see, and the actual cause of your pain or illness may very well be overlooked until it's too late.

To my mind, the way to fix that is to dismantle the fatphobic system that allows these things to happen. And to my brother's mind, it's to make people thinner.

One of my dearest friends, beautiful, brilliant Manon, still talks about a time fifteen years ago when she came to my parents' house for Passover dinner and spent the whole time feeling judged because of the size of her body and worrying that my family was going to try and stage an intervention. Did she feel extra self-conscious because she knew what they did for a living? Yes. Was she imagining that they all felt like they could fix her with the right diet and exercise plan? Unlikely.

My brother—whom I generally adore—has been working furiously on an app that does all the disordered things my brain already does. It counts calories and exercise, and it alerts you when you're consuming more calories than you're burning. He doesn't understand that for some people, once they hear this noise, it won't go away. It will ruin their relationship with food, and themselves.

I understand that he thinks that he's helping. But he doesn't understand why I think that he's not (or why I don't follow his businesses on social media. Or why I refer to his app as THE EATING DISORDER APP).

It's hard to recover in a world where diet culture is everywhere. Where body fat is villainized. Where weight loss is seen as the only option for anyone who isn't in a thin body, where being fat is seen as a personal failing, and where anti-fat bias is the last remaining socially acceptable form of discrimination (it's because we *care*…).

It's even harder to recover with a family who believes those things.

CHAPTER 52

I've stopped doing cardio.

The first day back on my elliptical machine felt amazing (like in those movies where the drug addict goes back to using heroin). And the second day felt pretty good too.

By day three, a familiar blanket of exhaustion had started to settle over my body. I would wake very early in the morning, checking the time to see if it was time to exercise yet. And when I was doing it, I kept checking the time to see when I could stop. There was no endorphin high. There was a tiny high when I finished, a moment where the anxiety that had been building up was satisfied, mixed with relief that it was done for the day. Also, in addition to not enjoying the cardio, I didn't feel like washing my hair again (the other dark side of exercise addiction that no one talks about).

I think a lot of the exhaustion stemmed from the fact that I wasn't using the elliptical instead of walking. I was doing both. I'd tell myself that I wasn't going to walk, and then I'd walk (almost like it's an addition?). So basically, I was training like an athlete, but with no sport, and no talent. It was affecting my free time, my energy level, and obviously my hair. But probably also my metabolism. I'm finding the more I push my body, the more it clings onto every calorie. This is in complete contrast to the good old days where I could restrict for a few days, crank up the exercise and drop a few pounds without batting an eyelash.

The fact that I wasn't losing weight while doing the elliptical machine started to really get to me. I noticed a very intense desire to restrict, as though the exercise neural pathway and the restriction neural pathway are connected. My brain knows that the only reason that I'd do the elliptical at this point is for weight loss, and my brain also knows that a good way to lose weight is to eat less.

Brain:	Don't eat that.
Me:	Why not? I was fine eating this two days ago.
Brain:	But now you are doing cardio again! Why else would you use that bullshit machine but to lose weight?
Me:	It makes me feel better about my body and it gives me energy and…
Brain:	And?
Me:	Okay, yeah. I'm trying to lose weight.
Brain:	Right! So don't eat that!
Me:	But I'm in recovery. I need to eat that.
Brain:	Haha. Good one. If you are trying to lose weight you aren't in recovery.
Me:	I'm just trying to EXERCISE to lose weight, and you know, be healthy.
Brain:	Rolls eyes
Me:	Rolls eyes
Brain:	If you want to lose weight, I can help you with that. But you can't eat the way you have been eating. You need to cut out things like sugar again, for starters, and anything extra and unnecessary. You know this.
Me:	I don't know why I can't exercise first, to see if that works.

Brain:　　　　Because it won't. And because you know that there
　　　　　　　is a better way.

Me:　　　　　You are starting to sound a lot like my ED.

Brain:　　　　Well of course. You summoned me [takes off fake
　　　　　　　moustache].

The first few days after I stopped were really, really rough. Now that
it's been about ten days, I feel okay, and a little glad that I got it
out of my system and stopped the spiral before I got caught up in
it again.

　　I still don't feel ready to sell or dismantle my elliptical machine.
I have a fantasy that one day I might enjoy cardio in the way that
I used to, or in the way I like to believe that I used to. And maybe
I'm not quite ready to let it go. But for the foreseeable future, I'm
going to try to stay off it. I'm relieved it didn't work out (ugh! Pun
unintentional, but I'm leaving it). I'm relieved that I was able to
recognize it for the anorexia horcrux that it is. I'm relieved that
in this instance I was stronger than the ED. And I'm relieved that
I don't have to wash my hair again today.

CHAPTER 53

Are you waiting for the part where I really begin to understand that having a big life is more important than having a small body? Or the moment of epiphany where I realize it's just too platitudinous and gross and trite to keep questioning my recovery from anorexia because I'm worried about more weight gain?

Me too.

Things have definitely changed. I've stopped weighing my food and doing cardio. Today I had a latte because I wanted one more than I wanted black coffee.

Though I'm still calorie counting (even though the numbers are less precise these days), and walking too much, and letting a voice in my head boss me around. And I feel like I'm running out of time.

Emily thought we should take a break for a month. She wanted to see how many of the changes I could keep on my own. I don't think it's dissimilar to leaving the chiropractor and hoping your adjustment holds, but for me it felt like leaving the chiropractor mid-adjustment. I wasn't ready for a break.

And I feel bad for not being able to progress on my own. This is my recovery, it's for me. Why do I need an outside person to push me? Why am I not self-motivated?

I've been thinking a lot about my tendency to put off making certain changes until an unnamed future date. When I had little babies, strangers would come up to me and say things like "the days are long, but the years are short." And in the moment, when there was spit-up down my back, and smashed peas in my hair, and all I wanted was a shower and some sleep, I didn't know what they were talking about, or why they couldn't mind their own business (or offer to hold my baby so I could pee).

But they were right. You blink and rub your tired, dry eyes, and your baby has grown into a child.

This is true about having children and also true about life, and recovery.

The days are long, but the years are short.

Putting off the hard right thing makes the ED behavior more bearable in the moment (sure this walk in the icy rain is miserable, but soon I will stop compulsively walking, so I can do one more cold, wet, exhausting walk today). It's like I have made a silent agreement with my eating disorder to punish myself a certain amount, and then it will let me know when I'm done. Though obviously that doesn't work.

There is no magic switch.

It will never feel easy.

It will never be the exact right time.

I've been putting off making the hardest changes for tomorrow, but then the tomorrows all blend together. I need to do the next right thing every time I'm faced with a decision. I don't want to look back and realize that I've run out of time.

The little micro decisions add up to a life.

CHAPTER 54

I keep expecting recovery to happen while controlling my weight.

I expect my exercise addiction to go away while stopping almost all of it, but not quite everything.

I expect my body hatred to go away while body checking and beating myself up for every discernible change

I expect the ED to relinquish control, while still letting it control me.

None of that even makes sense.

From now on, I vow to see my changing body as a step toward freedom, and recovery.

I will stop berating myself for breaking away from the ED.

I will try to treat myself with the same kindness I would bestow on any stranger.

I will remember that desperately trying to stay the same is what has kept me stuck.

CHAPTER 55

Decisions are very hard for me. I cogitate and vacillate and then even after I've chosen something, I can't help thinking about all the reasons I should have done the other thing.

That's why I have always had a lot of sympathy for the Bachelorette trying to narrow it down the day before her definitely-not-contrived engagement.

Similarly, there was a time not that long ago that I was seeing three people at once: two recovery coaches and one psychologist. I was the Bachelorette, but rather than courting potential mates, I was courting coaches and therapists. How did this happen you might ask? Obviously, the usual way.

After my break with Emily, I decided to try a new coach. Not because of Emily, but because I thought that maybe I needed a change. This was hard for a bunch of reasons, but mostly because of how great Emily is. She's astute and thoughtful and knowledgeable, and really *gets it*. But we had been working together for a long time, and I couldn't help but wonder if I needed to try something completely different. I felt like she was growing impatient, and I'd started lying to her because I was afraid of doing the things I'd agreed to do but was more afraid of not agreeing to do them or telling her I couldn't do them. Something had to give.

I signed up with a relatively well-known coach [Bachelorette #1] who claims that she can help everyone. Even people who have been ill longer than me (does such a person exist?) and who are as stubborn as I am (this person can't possibly exist). Her whole thing is being able to identify the eating-disorder voice and talk back to it. Which means spending entire sessions dialoguing with the voices in your head ("*what does eating disorder self think of that? What does healthy self think?*"). I wanted to find this practice helpful, but the truth is that no matter how the dialogue started (I'm afraid to eat the thing! I'm afraid to stop exercising! I feel guilty for having eaten the thing! I feel guilty for not exercising!), every dialogue ended the exact same way. My fears always came down to worrying that I won't be able to recover or that I will end up gaining a bunch of weight and being judged for that by everyone, especially myself. And there was no dialoguing myself out of those fears. I also found it really hard not to make the ED voice funny or sarcastic.

I never connected with this coach, and I'm not sure whose fault that was (so I think we should probably blame her). I didn't take the dialoguing homework as seriously as I should have because I found it repetitive and tiresome. And the coach often canceled at the last minute or showed up late and didn't make up the time at the end (my work ethic was better at my teenage fast-food job). Although her social-media persona is someone who is quite warm and empathetic, I never felt like she cared if I recovered or not. She'd assign challenges and forget what she assigned. She'd assign writing assignments and never follow up. The times I tried to tell her I didn't think I was making progress, she argued with me (apparently, I'm not equipped to make that call). I left my sessions with her feeling either bad about myself (because of how she'd made me feel) or bad about her (because of how she'd made me feel). Oh, and I think she thought she was funnier than me (read: she was basically a monster).

The problem was that she was helpful-adjacent. I often left a session with her feeling like we were on the verge of touching on something that could be meaningful—unless I left the session feeling frustrated, because she didn't ask if there was something I wanted to talk about. Or bad because she didn't make eye contact, and so I was worried that she hated me. Or irritated that what was supposed to be an hour session only lasted for forty-two minutes for the second week in a row. Or irritated because she canceled at the last minute. Or irritated because she didn't show up.

About three weeks after I started seeing Bachelorette #1, I was ready to break up with her. Next, I booked a free consult with another coach who had come highly recommended by a friend. The consult went well (she made eye contact and asked me questions about my life!), so I signed on with her with the intention of breaking it off with Bachelorette #1. The catch? She only takes people who will commit to a block of eight sessions. And so I did.

Then my appointment with Bachelorette #1 came around and I couldn't end it. She told me that she thought I could recover, and that *she* could help me get there. I was so worried that I might miss out on something life changing if I broke up with her too soon—she's great at sales, constantly talking about all the people she has helped recover—that I stayed with this woman because of FOMO, recovery edition.

So I told Bachelorette #2 that I hadn't managed to break it off with Bachelorette #1, and she said that it was okay (I had already paid for the eight sessions). But I didn't tell Bachelorette #1 that I was contemplating taking someone else to the fantasy suite.

Bachelorette #2 is lovely. Soft-spoken, tender-hearted, and so very earnest. None of which is my brand. She doesn't really joke, or get *my* jokes, and when I told her that I'm funny, she didn't seem to believe me (and that was the day that I learned that there is nothing less funny than trying to persuade someone that you are funny). She did however keep asking me about my "stand-up routine" after that. And while I realize that recovery isn't one big laugh-fest, jokes are how I relate to people and cope with tension. Humor is my most important language.

I really wanted to make it work, but I couldn't. Every week I'd go into our session hoping we would make a breakthrough and I'd walk away frustrated that we hadn't, and that I couldn't end things until my sessions were used up.

Then my name came up on a waiting list for a psychologist who specialized in EDs that I'd put myself on two-and-a-half years earlier. I actually almost said no to this one (FOMO be damned!) because I knew this particular psychologist from the day hospital program and was pretty sure that it wouldn't work out. But the receptionist convinced me there was no harm in trying one session; after all I had been on the waiting list longer than the lifespan of most network sitcoms (and some hedgehogs! I know, they are so cute, it's so sad!). The session went exactly as expected (fine, but I didn't feel particularly understood) so I decided not to go back. And then the psychologist called me and asked if I was sure. And if there is one thing that you can always count on with me, it's that I'm never sure about anything. Ever. She convinced me to give therapy with her a shot. So I agreed.

To recap, at this point I'm seeing two recovery coaches and one psychologist and I'm making very little progress, but I'm petrified to break up with any of them in case they hold the magic key to my recovery (Bachelorette #1 is so weirdly inexpensive that it makes my indecision mostly affordable). My walking has ramped back up, my food challenges are ridiculous (I'm just repeating things I worked on with Emily and I'm terrified of anything slightly out of my comfort zone), and I'm feeling defeated.

The first day of July is sunny and warm, and we have friends over for an afternoon swim and cocktails, which bleeds into dinner and drinks, and they stay longer than anyone had anticipated. This is mostly fine, because they are all fun and funny and the weather is spectacular. But it also means I spend the last two hours trying to work out how I'm going to fit in my long walk, which I'd put off that morning to prepare for our guests. Sitting still feels progressively agonizing, and I'm distracted thinking about movement and distracted thinking about how distracted I am. I laugh and smile and make jokes, and pour drinks and serve dessert, as the noise in my head reaches a crescendo.

After they leave, my husband and I put the kids to bed. I'm meant to be going to a get-together at my brother's. It's a balmy night, and the air smells like the beginning of summer and long weekend barbeques. I try to ignore the guilt and disappointment as I walk away from his house in the direction of my normal walking route. I walk quickly into the woods. It doesn't matter that I have terrible night vision and that the woods are dark (and that I walk by several groups blasting questionable, illegal fireworks), it doesn't matter that I'm missing a happy backyard party at my brother's, it doesn't matter that I've broken a commitment and chosen exercise over people, it doesn't matter that I've lied to my husband about where I'm going. It doesn't matter that—once again—I'm choosing my disorder over my actual life, and people I love. I start to cry. I can't stop, or turn back, or cut my walk short. I walk for three hours and go home, defeated, and, also, relieved.

The next day I email Emily and tell her that I'm ready to work on the walking. She writes back and says she will only take me back on the condition that I stop walking completely (and basically stop fucking around). I take two weeks to think about it.

Breaking up with everyone is as hard and annoying as it is on the actual Bachelorette. Well, except for Bachelorette #2, I simply let our sessions run out. Bachelorette #3 is so hard to break up with that I end up seeing her for about eight extra weeks because she is so hurt every time I suggest that we aren't a good fit. Finally, after a very expensive pep talk ("you are great! It's not you, it's me"), she releases me with the offer that I can come back any time.

Bachelorette #1 is a breakup befitting the show. She is petty and childish and tries to withhold money for a session I'd paid for in advance and she'd missed without notice. Her behavior is shocking, and confusing, but also the actual best—because it gets rid of any lingering recovery-coach FOMO. I have never been so confident about my decision to dump anyone, ever. My only concern is for the people she is still coaching.

I accept Emily's condition to give up the only form of exercise I have left. I'm anxious and angry and sad and teary and resentful and scared and a little bit hopeful.

I don't know if it's the timing, or five months of seeing other people, but going back to Emily this time is different. This is the part where everything starts to shift.

CHAPTER 56

The first time I tried to give up walking it was for five days, and I was still using my home elliptical machine (a piece of gym-grade cardio equipment that cost significantly more than my first car) every morning. This was a few months after I'd accepted I still had a pretty serious problem with food and exercise, but a few months before I'd start with Emily for the first time.

After weeks and weeks of talking about it with my then-therapist, I decided I'd stop walking for one work week, which Kirsten quickly branded the "No-Walkathon". I chose a week that my kids would be in camp across town because I had to drive back and forth three times a day (my youngest finished at 1, while my two other kids finished at 4, and no, I don't know what I was thinking at sign-up time). I figured I had a built-in distraction—rush-hour traffic in the height of construction season is basically nature's TV, I'm sure I've seen that on an inspirational postcard. It also felt like as good a week as any because I was already anticipating a fair amount of distress owing to all of the forced driving (when I'm driving, I can't be walking).

The first two mornings I ran errands by car, and in the evenings, Kirsten saved me. She showed up at my house with wine both nights, the second night finding me frantically pacing in my family room (she'd used the back door and saw me through the window). She didn't believe my lie that I was breaking in new shoes (because I wasn't wearing any), and I was deeply embarrassed in front of this person who knows every one of my secrets. I was so grateful to have her there, but also so ashamed, because we both knew that it was more than a social call.

On day three I made it through the morning by sitting on my friend Amy's backyard deck. Amy was the only person other than Kirsten whom I'd told about any of it at that point, mostly because she's a very caring person and a doctor with great instincts who'd already guessed that something was up and relentlessly asked me questions about my health until I told her. That night I had plans to go for drinks at a downtown patio with high school friends, and I told myself (and Kirsten) I'd Uber both ways. Then—as she's always done—one of my friends asked to park at my place so we could catch up on the walk there (I live about 2.5 miles from the patio in question and she lives approximately eleventy-billion, or however far the suburbs are). Because saying no to friends is something I struggle with anyway, and because exercise is something I'm addicted to, I agreed to the walk, promising myself I'd explain all of it on the way there and that we'd Uber home.

The decision to tell her was hard, despite our thirty-five-year friendship. She's a doctor, like Amy, but she's very into diet culture and exercise, and I was pretty sure she wouldn't get it. Additionally, it would be the first time we'd discuss my eating disorder since I was hospitalized and had needed her to grab a math textbook and strawberry Lip Smackers from my locker. She had witnessed the first diet, the slippery descent into illness, the grade eight grad, the water-loading, the hospitalizations, the hasty move out of my parents' house, the breakup with Rick, the crushing betrayal of the family business, the ovulation drugs, the loss of appetite, the accidental weight loss, the tibial facture, and the osteopenia. But we had never *talked* about any of it.

I was right. She didn't really understand the point of the No-Walkathon (though I'm sure I didn't do an amazing job explaining it—I've had the awful out-of-body experience of hearing myself ramble awkwardly). I was also a little hurt after I finally found the courage and the words to say that I wasn't really better, and she casually said our whole group of friends was already aware. Could none of them have let me in on the secret? Also, I wanted to know how she knew that. Had they been *talking* about me behind my back? How frequently? When did it come up? Was it only when they were choosing restaurants or were they watching me not-eat at social engagements? I thought back to all of the gatherings at everyone's homes over the years, and suddenly understood why everyone always had a vegetable tray out and made a point of showing me where it was, like flight attendants pointing out the fire exits.

At the end of the night my friend asked if I wanted to Uber home, but I knew that she wanted to walk (let's face it, I did too), so we did. When I reported back to Kirsten, she wasn't terribly surprised and mentioned that I should have accepted her offer to come sit in her backyard that night instead. Apparently, she wasn't privy to my two-consecutive-days-of-help-maximum rule.

On Thursday I had to take my kids to a birthday party after camp. And holy crap, was I cranky. At least three people made comments about the fact I hadn't walked there with my kids (is that your CAR Sheri? Do you DRIVE?), and the party itself was a nightmare with a singing princess + crafts + a bouncy castle + a swimming component + an art component. And a meal. And cake. And ice cream. If you are wondering how someone can possibly cram all. that. fun. into a reasonable party, the answer is that you cannot. It was the never-ending party. After over four torturous hours of being splashed by pool water, sprayed with paint, and sprinkled with fairy princess glitter, we were the first to leave.

My husband was out of town, and my kids were too young for me to go anywhere without them. So, after they went to bed I got changed and went upstairs to use my home elliptical machine and did my second long workout of the day. I had failed.

On Friday I drove to a friend's place for a swim with my kids and was distracted the entire time by the fact that we hadn't walked, and that my friend was so surprised to see my car. That night I went for a walk. I was done. I was frazzled and weepy and shocked by the magnitude of my problem—and by how many parking tickets I'd managed to accumulate over the course of four days (did you know that the parking rules change from hour to hour based on *signs* on the street?).

When I started with Emily in September, two months after the No-Walkathon, we addressed the walking very slowly, making gradual reductions while I was still using the elliptical machine. In hindsight, I can't believe how hard that felt. I was still doing cardio! Why was I acting like it was the end of the world?

My next No-Walkathon happened seven months after Emily and I started, over the course of three consecutive days. Kevin spent the entire three days with me, morning to night, and gave up drinking for those days as a show of solidarity (and out of obligation I gave up drinking to show solidarity with his generous show of solidarity, which didn't help anyone's mood). When it was over, we celebrated by walking to a bar.

Then, this past December, two-and-a-half years after the original No-Walkathon and nine months after quitting my daily cardio workouts, I made an agreement with Emily that I'd spend one whole day at home, no exercise, no walks. I'd been training (not-training!) for that day for months, gradually reducing my walking a little more every week. Though I'd never done a day of absolutely no movement—even cottage visits involved some degree of walking around—and I didn't think I could do it. So when the day came, and I did it, I couldn't believe it. I felt so incredibly proud, and so incredibly guilty (in this kind of recovery, victory is often accompanied by crushing guilt and fear and self-doubt).

Emily and I took a break six weeks later, and it wasn't long before I was back to where I'd started. I accepted a drive home from yoga one day because Elizabeth refused to take no for an answer, and then as soon as she was far enough away from my house, I walked back to the studio so that I could walk home. I couldn't drive anywhere I deemed walkable, and my characterization of "walkable" had become so ridiculous that I couldn't tell people where I walked. Friends would call sometimes and on hearing traffic in the background ask where I was and I couldn't tell them the truth. One friend who didn't understand the severity of the issue (because I'd never told her), and frequently talked about how much she admired how active I was, pestered me to show everyone the step count on my phone at drinks one night, and I refused because it was so ridiculously high. I was so embarrassed. And I couldn't stop.

When a genome study came out a couple of years ago showing that anorexia and OCD have a higher genetic correlation than any other two psychiatric disorders, I was about as surprised as I was to learn that Kim Kardashian isn't 100 percent natural.

I've never experienced OCD, but my movement compulsion feels exactly the way I expect OCD must feel. I go out thinking I'll run a quick errand, and before I know it, I've taken the long way home and wasted two hours. Or I say that I'll go the shorter way, and I can't make myself turn toward home. Or I leave my house with a plan to walk to the closest dollar store only to find myself walking to one six neighborhoods away, and it takes up my entire afternoon. However, as I understand it, a notable difference is that with OCD when people stop the behavior, for example excessive handwashing, the terrible consequence they fear almost never happens. A lot of my fear around not walking enough is because I'm afraid of gaining weight, which has actually happened and will likely continue to happen until my body settles. So now I'm counting on the fear about all the horrible ways extra weight will impact my life as being the scary thing that never comes true.

I'd never given any serious thought to stopping walking until I realized that I was out of options. Even before I contacted Emily this last time, I knew what she was going to say, and I knew I was going to accept her conditions. I knew I couldn't hold onto my exercise addiction in any form and recover.

The first week, Emily and I agreed that I'd walk absolutely nowhere. I had to drive to the pharmacy three blocks away and to the mall and to my kids' pediatrician and to the grocery store. My brother, who didn't know about my recovery, let alone the No-Walkathon, kept asking me to go for walks with him and my niece (an Australian Labradoodle) and saying no made me cry. Luckily, we were texting.

It felt so unfair and punishing. I can rationalize food challenges much of the time (normal people can eat salad dressing. Normal people can eat buttered vegetables. Normal people can eat cake. Normal people can eat a sandwich) but it's harder with walking. Everyone walks (except Kirsten, whose recovery silver lining was never having to agree to walk anywhere with me ever again). But I did it. And the next week, I did it again. And the week after that, I did it again.

It's been over four solid months of drastically reduced walking. I'm now allowed to walk my kids to school and to walk to the grocery store and the pharmacy, but not twice in the same day. I'm also usually allowed two "walking days" per week (which I feel is on par with many maximum-security prisoners, so not a terrible deal). I'd like to say that it feels fine now, and that I'm used to it and that I love the extra time that it allows me in my day, and that I never fuck it up, but that would be a lie. Some days I appreciate the extra time and that I don't have to walk in the rain or when I'm ill or when I'm injured. I appreciate that I can accept a drive home and not have to secretly retrace my steps and that I can drive to the grocery store. And some days I want to walk so badly it's all I can think about—I do other things, but they are sepia and the urge to move is bright red. Yesterday I went for a walk on a day that I wasn't supposed to, because in the moment, I couldn't remember why I was doing any of it. I felt fat and sad and guilty and hopeless, and I was jealous of people I saw running outside and people with Pelotons (like vegans and people who eat kale, someone who has a Peloton will always let you know they have one). I was jealous of every gym-goer, and every single person with a dog (except for those ones you have to carry in your purse). And when I told Emily about it, she understood, and she reminded me that I'm not doing any of this to be like everyone else, or to look like everyone else, I'm doing it to make my life different and better. Today I didn't walk. I still feel sad and guilty and uncomfortable, but a little less hopeless. And kind of proud.

CHAPTER 57

I am at my highest non-pregnancy weight ever. I'm closer to the weight I was when I gave birth than I am to the weight I've been sitting at since my mid-twenties. I'm ten pounds higher than my discharge weight at the children's hospital (which I never got anywhere close to, because of expert water-loading), and I'm only two pounds below the goal weight set by the day hospital program. But I'm not recovered because goal weights aren't magic, and the fact that they exist keeps many of us stuck. We are wont to see them as the endpoint, not the beginning. This is why so many people end up settling for a version of quasi-recovery or relapsing. You get to your goal weight, and the noise is louder than ever, but you feel like you have to maintain that weight because it's your goal—you are supposed to be recovered now. And it's hell, because you are too fat for anorexia and you are not quite fat enough to be recovered.

In case there is any ambiguity, I am deeply uncomfortable. I am uncomfortable enough that I try not to look at my body in the mirror because when I do, I feel bad for hours. I am uncomfortable enough that some days I have to change three times before I leave the house. I am uncomfortable enough that a clothes shopping trip can make me weepy, and many nights when I wake up in the middle of the night to pee, I can't fall back asleep because the words "what have I done" are so loud, they keep me awake (yes, I really *should* stop consuming all liquids by 10).

I've also started to accept the cruel paradox that the only way I'll ever be comfortable with my body is by gaining more weight.

In order to appease the angry noise coming from my eating disorder right now, I'll also add that I can be comfortable in my body again if I lose weight (There! Happy you annoying demon?). The problem with that of course is that I'll be stuck in the eating disorder forever, all this work will have been for nothing. I'll fit back into all my old clothes, but I'll never learn that the way my body looks isn't the most important thing about me. And as I continue to age and my body inevitably keeps changing, I will experience the same distress over and over. I will also know on some level that I failed, and that things might have been different.

If I gain weight, I will continue to be uncomfortable. And then the hope is I'll get used to it. But staying here, on the steepest part of the mountain, five meters or five kilometers from the summit (who knows which), is untenable. Right now, in this place that looks like health to everyone around me, I'm dealing with more noise and distress than I ever did in the depths of illness, because I'm breaking rules all the time, and I've gained weight, and there is no relief. I can't stay here.

Every account of true, full, robust recovery that I know of has involved people who allowed their bodies to go beyond "recovered" goal weights, because goal weights are usually not high enough. Those of us who can't get past the idea that goal weights are a *minimum* and not a maximum stay there. And we remain ill.

It's illogical that people are expected to recover at the lowest healthy weight for their height based on the BMI, a nonsense-standard never intended to be used as a measure of individual health but rather invented by a mathematician to measure obesity at a population level two hundred years ago. To put this in perspective, *bloodletting* was also considered scientifically sound two hundred years ago.

Even if we were to pretend that the BMI wasn't pseudo-science, and that it took things like race, muscle mass, body diversity, age (and *science*) into account, the way goal weights are determined still doesn't make sense. If you think about the way a bell curve works, and the way human beings look, it's pretty obvious that most people won't land at the very bottom of the bell curve when they are at their natural unsuppressed body weights. And yet, that's where goal weights tend to be set.

This probably happens for a whole slew of reasons, some legitimate and some less so. One generally accepted reason is that medical professionals don't want to scare us. If you had told me at the beginning of recovery that I'd be this close to my goal weight and this certain that I won't fully recover at this weight, I'd have run away screaming (I'm not being hyperbolic. I have vivid memories of running away screaming from the children's hospital more than once, and it's not like I've really matured since then). However, as I've gained weight, my thinking has changed. I can now see why a few extra pounds are worth it, if it's the difference between quasi-recovery and full freedom from my eating disorder and all. that. noise.

Another reason goal weights are set so low is because there is a shortage of resources. Insurance companies don't want to pay any longer than they have to, and hospitals need beds and spots in programs. Finally, doctors don't want us to end up "overweight" any more than our eating disorders do. Sometimes that's because they are worried we won't be able to deal with it, and sometimes it's because they are fatphobic. Often both.

A study that's very well-known in recovery circles, but apparently not super-popular cocktail party patter, is the Minnesota Starvation Experiment. The 1944–1945 wartime experiment, led by a scientist by the name of Ancel Keys, was designed to study the psychological and physiological effects of starvation to identify potential complications associated with refeeding civilians who had been starved during the war. The participants, thirty-six conscientious objectors who chose semi-starvation over enlisting, were examined and proclaimed to be extremely physically and psychologically fit prior to being accepted into the study.

The study involved four phases: a twelve-week maintenance phase where the participants' daily intake was adjusted to maintain caloric balance for each person's particular body; a six-month weight-loss phase where the men lost on average 25 percent of their normal bodyweight through a combination of physical activity and severely calorically restricted diets (think *The Biggest Loser*); a twelve-week restrictive rehabilitation period where calories were increased in increments; and finally an unrestricted rehabilitation period where one-third of the men volunteered to stay for an extra eight weeks and ate freely without any caloric limits.

Some of the most notable findings to come out of this study from a recovery standpoint were that the men all developed many of the physical and psychological symptoms associated with anorexia during both the starvation period and the controlled refeeding period, including obsessive thoughts, increased anxiety and depressive symptoms, and feelings of increased fullness and discomfort after eating. The other thing worth noting is that the men on average gained ten percent more than their pre-starvation weights before their metabolism, thoughts, and hunger levels went back to normal. In almost all cases the men's weights eventually returned to their original pre-starvation weights, but the salient point is that the men wouldn't have cared whether they did; they simply wanted to feel better. Without anorexia holding them back, they had enough presence of mind to let their bodies do what was necessary to heal. Had they not allowed their bodies to get to that place, their metabolisms would have remained suppressed, and their thoughts would have remained rigid and obsessive.

I'm constantly surprised (disappointed) by the number of treatment professionals who take it for granted that full recovery is an impossible fantasy, like a really good *Friday Night Lights* reboot.

I recently talked with a dietician about a video she uses to train other dietitians to work with people with eating disorders. In this video there is a "recovered" woman who says that her eating disorder will always be sitting on her left shoulder but that she turns toward it less often. I was so annoyed that this was a certified eating disorder professional's definition of *full recovery* that I almost laughed out loud. The woman in the video could have been me. That is the exact same type of nonsense I would have told people before this recovery effort (if I were ever forced to talk about my history of anorexia, like maybe in a hostage-type situation). I told the dietician that if I thought my eating disorder was going to be hanging out on my shoulder for the rest of my life, I wouldn't be making myself this uncomfortable. I'd be keeping my body in a place where the eating disorder on my shoulder would be less cranky and yelly. I also told her that the woman in the video is not recovered, and as such shouldn't be making videos about recovery (that aren't cautionary tales). I also dumped the dietician.

I am so grateful to know people, and know of people, who are fully recovered and to have read the accounts they've written. I wish all treatment professionals understood that setting goal weights too low, and calling people recovered before their minds have healed, is like taking a cast off someone's leg before the bone has set—either they will end up limping for the rest of their life or breaking the bone again.

So now, I'm working hard to let go of the idea that a predetermined goal weight is my end point. Like the men in the Minnesota Starvation Experiment, I need to let my body get where it needs to be. And I'm so afraid. Afraid of judgment. Afraid it won't work. Afraid I can't get there.

But I'm more afraid of stopping too soon and having an eating disorder on my left shoulder for the rest of my life.

CHAPTER 58

The first time I ran away, I was about five or six, and I hid in my backyard and came in when I got hungry. It was the olden days, I was one of three kids, and no one noticed.

The second time I ran away I was about sixteen and inpatient at the children's hospital. It was Easter weekend, so skeleton staff, and my roommate Katy (a teeny tiny blonde bulimic who always had a massive wad of gum in her mouth) and I were downstairs heading to the gift shop when we saw a city bus through the window. We ran outside and hopped on through the back doors with no real knowledge of where the bus was headed. Eventually we got to a familiar mall, got off and walked around. It was the taste of freedom—and rebellion—we both needed, and we decided to return to the hospital in time for dinner (read: neither of us had any money).

The third time was a failed attempt. I must have been seventeen as that's the age you can sign yourself out of the hospital. I had just been weighed and was told I was to be on bed rest for what was probably the fourth day in a row. Confused (*I'd been eating, why the actual hell was I still losing weight?*) and inconsolable (I. can't. spend. one. more. day. all. alone. in. my. room.), I told the nurse to give me back my clothing and possessions that had been boxed up the first day I was on bed rest and that I was signing myself out *thankyouverymuch*. I then asked to use the phone at the nurses' station—the one in my room had been taken away with the rest of my stuff—and I called my parents to see if they would come get me. They said no (the only surprise here is that I was surprised). Then I called my friend Andrea, my only friend with a car, and she said yes. I got dressed. My parents called Andrea's parents to make sure they knew I wasn't allowed to go to my home and that I certainly wasn't allowed to stay at Andrea's home. Her parents liked me a lot (and were also very fatphobic, frequently asking Andrea why she couldn't look like me, and therefore would have likely been on board with my desire to leave the hospital before I got fat), but they understood the adult-code and told Andrea that they couldn't go against my parents' wishes. When Andrea called to tell me about this new development, I asked her to come anyway, envisioning a life on the street as preferable to another day of bed rest (in my defense, I'd led a pretty sheltered life). By the time Andrea showed up, my doctor had been called and was threatening to sign papers forcing a three-day involuntary hold. Given that I had nowhere to go and that I didn't want to be placed on a psychiatric hold—my bed had always been on a medical ward, not psych—I got back into my inelegant light yellow hospital gown and striped flannel hospital pyjama pants and hopped back into bed. In happy news, it killed most of what would have otherwise been a very long, dull morning on bed rest.

In grade twelve my parents and I agreed I'd attend a twice-weekly psycho-educational group at the adult hospital in lieu of treatment at the children's. The group consisted of women who, at the time, seemed ancient but who were on average probably ten years younger than I am now (so, very young and spry). The group was interesting enough, but it was mainly dominated by one woman who talked incessantly about her inability to stop binging and purging. Every week we'd get photocopied handouts of articles explaining why starving yourself is very bad, and why purging is also very bad. Needless to say, I wasn't cured by photocopy ink-osmosis, and toward the end of grade twelve—an otherwise super-fun year uninterrupted by any hospital stays when I was able to play the lead in a community production of West Side Story, join a pretty exclusive local theater group, and dabble in professional acting jobs—my parents said I had to start going back to the children's hospital for weigh-ins. I said no. They said that if I didn't go back to treatment that I couldn't live with them anymore. I moved into a dingy downtown basement apartment on July 1.

That was the last time I felt like a part of my parents' family.

I don't know if living on my own in my last year of high school made any difference as far as my eating disorder was concerned. My eating disorder did probably affect my relationship with my new roommates though, university students I met at my part-time retail job. I wouldn't share food, or meals, or drinks, and briefly went through a period when I was throwing up nearly everything I ate, which I'm sure they knew because we shared one bathroom. This was something I found scary and uncontrollable (I wasn't shoving my fingers down my throat, but I also made no effort to stop it from happening) and I've never discussed with anyone to this day. It is however worth noting that the timing was rather unfortunate, given the bathroom-to-people ratio.

The truth is that illness aside, I was too young to be living with those girls who had frequent loud boozy parties, brought horny inebriated strangers home from bars, and didn't have to get up for high school every morning. I remember listening to Enya on my Walkman (young people: picture a small battery-operated square yellow box that did nothing but play music that came in a smaller rectangle box) at night in bed, trying to drown out drunk laughter so that I could fall asleep. I honestly can't remember if I ever felt homesick, but I keep thinking that I must have (right?).

One day I went into the kitchen (something I didn't do every day) and found a pot of spaghetti sauce on the stove so old it had white circles of mold on the surface. Completely fed up with my roommates and their seeming inability to clean anything, ever, I took the entire pot and put it outdoors. When the owner of the pot found out, she was furious. And she called me anorexic. It was the meanest, most hurtful thing she could have called me. It was a slur. After that I stayed away as much as I could, which wasn't hard given how busy I was going to school, working, acting, rehearsing, exercising and eventually applying to university.

Meanwhile, my parents and siblings grew closer as a family, which felt like confirmation that I was the problem they needed to get rid of. It reinforced the feeling I'd had since childhood that I was the thing standing in the way of the family they'd always wanted. First it was my chubbiness ruining photos and the perfect-family aesthetic, and then it was my illness. It didn't matter what I achieved at school, or how many friends I had, or how many times I played the lead, or how many awards I got, or how many of my mom's friends thought I was pretty, I felt like I was the thing keeping them from happiness and ruining everything, and that my moving out fixed all of that. My mom stopped speaking to me for three months that spring because I chose to rehearse with my school improv team the night before the national championship instead of attending a Passover Seder (since everyone is *clearly* wondering I'll add that my team won the nationals!). It was the first time my mother would completely freeze me out for any meaningful length of time, but absolutely not the last, and it felt like a very clear message that I was completely dispensable, if not disposable.

I'm pretty confident that it was a huge relief for my parents to have me out of the house. I'm not saying this with self-pity or bitterness. As a parent, I can see that living with a child who has anorexia has to be impossibly hard, and stressful, and exhausting, and I have a lot of sympathy for them now. And I understand why

they needed time to heal their family. It also makes me really sad
though. Occasionally they still talk about their trip to Boston (a trip
I only found out about when I saw a framed photo of them all on my
mother's dresser) and other fun things they did as a family, and I wish
that things could have been different, and that I could have been less
broken, and easier to parent. Though I also don't know what I could
have done differently; I never chose to get sick. So I'm choosing to
forgive myself too.

CHAPTER 59

If you were to ask me how to recover from a restrictive eating disorder, I might not have had an answer for you a few months ago. But I've figured it out. Seriously. We can basically throw out the rest of this book. Sorry for wasting your time with all of the reading to this point.

I honestly feel like it can be boiled down to two things, and they are as follows: commitment and sitting with discomfort. That's the whole thing. Committing and sitting (do you like that as a catchphrase? Should I workshop it a little more?).

Commitment is important because you will want to quit a lot, more than anyone who isn't in it can possibly fathom. You will want to quit when you look in the mirror. You will want to quit when you try on clothes. You will want to quit when you wake up in a panic in the middle of the night more nights than you don't. You will want to quit when you feel too full. You will want to quit when your friends are talking about exercise and juice fasts, and you are forcing yourself to be still and eat things that scare you. Commitment means wanting to quit but remembering your promise to yourself that you won't. Commitment means making a promise in your right mind and knowing that the part of you that will try to persuade you to quit doesn't have your best interests at heart.

This brings us to the other tool you will need. You will need to learn to sit with discomfort. If you can't, you won't be able to do any of the things needed to recover. Recovery is more uncomfortable than that time your friend in law school convinced you to try thong underwear and you wore them all day because it didn't occur to you that you could *take them off.* Recovery is more uncomfortable than that guy you ghosted after two dates coming into your hospital room to see how many centimeters dilated you are. Recovery is more uncomfortable than that time you skipped out of a breakfast seminar at a work retreat to get a workout in and realized that your boss and all your colleagues were in the room overlooking the hotel gym. Recovery is the most uncomfortable thing you will ever do because it involves all your senses, and because for it to work you have to be uncomfortable more than you are not.

Let's take an average morning in recovery. You wake up feeling flabby or lazy or anxious and you desperately want a workout. So instead of that you go make yourself breakfast (sorry exercise endorphins, you aren't invited!). Instead of the breakfast you always used to eat, you have eggs and buttered toast. You struggle through making it (how much butter is a normal amount? Do I have to butter the pan *and* the toast? Can I measure the butter? Can I use artificial sweetener in my tea?) but because you are committed to recovery, you make the breakfast you planned to make when you got into the kitchen, and you eat it. You don't let your eating disorder hijack your plan.

After breakfast, you shower and get dressed. Maybe you don't like what you see when you get undressed to shower. Maybe you still have to resist the urge to exercise. Maybe you pull on a pair of pants that feel tighter than they did the last time you wore them, and the voice in your head reminds you that you know how to make yourself feel okay in those pants again. But you are committed to recovery, and you sit with the discomfort of being full, and of your clothes fitting differently, and of being still when you desperately want to move.

The more you do it, the more your tolerance for distress increases, like an elastic. Which means you can now do more uncomfortable things. When all the things are done, and you have practiced them enough times, you will recover.

Easy peezy lemon squeezy.

I don't think I understood either of these concepts at the beginning of this recovery effort. Maybe in part because my brain needed to be better nourished, and maybe because I wasn't ready yet. I don't know that anyone ever feels completely ready to recover, but you have to be prepared to go against what feels like your gut instincts constantly, to do the things that you have wired your brain to be terrified of over and over and over until they become less terrifying. You have to be prepared to keep going no matter how noisy it gets, with the understanding that eventually the noise will stop. Which is where neuroplasticity comes in.

The image that pops into my head when I think about neural rewiring is a snowy path in an arboretum near my house. People walk through there all winter long, and it's really easy to follow the path, even on the snowiest days. Creating a new neural pathway is equivalent to walking through the deep, heavy untouched snow day after day until a new path is formed. If you get complacent at the beginning and take the path that is already packed down by other people's footsteps and dog pee (let's say you don't butter your toast and quickly weigh your bread while no one is looking just to take the edge off), your new path will get snowed over pretty quickly again (you are showing your brain that you aren't committed to recovery). You must stay on the new path, no matter how exhausting, terrifying, demoralizing, painful it feels. You must remember what you committed to, and why.

None of this is simple. Though I really wonder if when I entered the day hospital program, if the very first lesson on the very first day had been about learning to sit with discomfort, if I could have more readily accepted that as a sign of healing. And maybe if I'd had a letter that I'd written to myself, committing to the process no matter how hard it got, I might not have run out that first time, and I might not have slipped up as many times as I did after that.

Maybe those were lessons I had to learn later. Maybe I needed to be reminded that being in an eating disorder is ultimately just as uncomfortable as recovery, even if it doesn't feel that way when I'm doing all the things that scare me. Maybe I had to be reminded of all of the things that I was missing or had missed. I had to not only want recovery, but I also had to believe in recovery. I had to believe that recovery is more than growing into a bigger body and keeping the same menacing thoughts. I had to believe that recovery could offer me mental freedom so far beyond my comprehension that I'm willing to jump blindly into the snow and keep trudging. But on the days I don't believe it, when the snow feels heavy and exhausting and I want to run back to the ease and comfort of my eating disorder, those are the days a really great catchphrase could come in handy.

I'm going to keep workshopping it.

CHAPTER 60

The first time Kirsten and I went out for a meal, shortly after I told her how scary meals were for me, it was somewhere fancy. I had finally filled her in on everything, and she was kinder and more understanding and mockier than I ever could have hoped. While it was obvious from the minute I told her that she was taking my recovery very seriously (more seriously than I was at many points), she was taking *me* as un-seriously as ever. It took less than twenty-four hours for the teasing to start, and that was exactly what I needed.

The waitress brought us each a complementary amuse bouche, which as far as we could tell was alcohol wrapped in hardened oil. I tried to say no thank you (oil being a food I'd avoided for most of my life), and Kirsten said, "She'll have one, thanks." And then she made me eat it using a combination of jokes and persuasion. By the time I put that thing in my mouth, I wasn't sure if the tears running down my face were borne of laughter or terror. The rest of that meal was truly awful. I was only just starting recovery, and it was the first time I'd put myself in a situation where I was planning to do things that were intentionally uncomfortable, and the first time I'd voluntarily let anyone other than my eating disorder choose what was going to go in my mouth. That day we established a pattern, whereby Kirsten was the boss of all food-things when we were together.

Kirsten was the perfect person to eat with because she loves food. She likes reading about it, and shopping for it and preparing it and eating it. She knows the best restaurant for everything, and if she doesn't, she will find it. There are a lot of people with eating disorders who love all those things too—many becoming so obsessed with all the food they will never eat that they pursue careers in the food industry, or prepare elaborate meals for family and friends, but sadly for my husband who certainly would have appreciated a gourmet homemade dinner from time to time, this was never one of my symptoms. I was content to eat the same safe foods over and over, meal after meal. I never felt like I was missing out on anything because food never felt important to me. Psychological comfort felt more important than food variety.

Kirsten and I had a lot of meals out. We'd meet for lunches, dinners, and snacks. She'd sit patiently while I sobbed over pasta and seconds later make me laugh so hard that I was sure I'd aspirated wine. She joked about me to waiters who made the mistake of asking how we liked our meals "don't ask her. She has no idea" or if we were ready to order "she'll never be ready but if you want to go home today, she'll do it now" and while from someone else I might have felt diminished, the fact that all of it came from a place of love made whispered comments like "the waiter thinks that you have an *extremely* low IQ" hilariously comforting.

Kirsten was the first person who made me feel understood (because she worked so incredibly hard to understand), and not ashamed of my eating disorder. It was because of the way she reacted when I told her that I was able to go on to tell other people, and it was because of her unconditional support that I was able to accept help from other people.

There is no way I would have made it through my fear foods list if it wasn't for her. Emily had given me a deadline, and because of how much I stalled and procrastinated I had to do approximately eight things in the last five days. Kirsten met me for about five of those meals.

When she moved from down the street to a city a four-hour drive away, I was devastated. I missed getting our nails done together, and seeing silly questionable movies, and drinking wine in the park, and Friday pizza with all our kids. I missed seeing her car illegally parked at school dropoff every morning and bumping into her when I was out running an errand. I stopped walking down my own street for over a year because seeing her house without her wreath on the door made me cry.

In addition to the heartbreak of her being gone, I had to learn how to do food challenges on my own. Kevin and Neil stepped up, but Kevin found lady-tears disconcerting, and I felt bad for him. Elizabeth stepped up but she didn't understand "Why are you crying? Are you worried you are going to get FAT? You know that's ridiculous, right?" Amy stepped up but she was *too* supportive: "You are doing amazing. You are so, so, so *brave*." My husband stepped up but wasn't sure how that worked "Are you going to eat that? I'll have it if you aren't." So I learned to do these things on my own, which was more important than I knew.

Sure, it's easier and better to do any of these things with a supportive person (though not too supportive a person!) but finally understanding I needed to be accountable to myself, was crucial.

With Kirsten, because I cared so much about pleasing her, disappointing her overshadowed everything. This was probably the pressure I needed at the time, but I also remember the worst part about walking out of the day hospital program being that I'd upset her, and crying inconsolably after she expressed genuine frustration when she caught me walking on a day I wasn't supposed to be. So from a recovery standpoint, I needed to take more responsibility for my own actions. I couldn't keep doing things only because Kirsten believed in me, I needed to start believing in myself too.

With that said, I don't think that mattered at the beginning. I needed to build up my confidence and to experience what it felt like to succeed at challenging my eating disorder. I wouldn't have been able to eat that hardened ball of fat and booze without her pushing me to do it. I wouldn't have tried the day hospital program the first time, or gone back the second. I likely wouldn't have attempted the No-Walkathon, or restaurant pasta, or scary cocktails. Though at a certain point, I had to be doing it for me. I had to want to save myself.

The last time I visited Kirsten, we went for brunch. The waitress was friendly and loquacious and joked with us for close to an hour while we chatted over coffee and decided what to order. When our food arrived, I immediately noticed my salad had dressing on it (still something I find very challenging), and I couldn't keep up with my racing thoughts. Do I keep it? Do I say something? Can I eat this? Will this ruin the rest of my day? What should I do?

The waitress noticed before I said anything and tried to take it back. "I'll get you a new one! I'm so sorry!" And Kirsten looked her straight in the eye and said, "She'll have this one." The waitress looked at me, then she looked at Kristen, then she looked at me.

Waitress:	Are you sure?
Kirsten:	She's sure [I nod].
Waitress:	It's no problem to get you a new one [she reaches for it].
Kirsten:	She's sure
Waitress:	This is so awkward [laughs nervously].
Me:	[voice finally working again] I'm sure! It's fine!
Waitress:	[speaking slowly in case I need to signal that I've been taken hostage by someone in the salad dressing cartel] Tell me if you change your mind...okay?

I gave her my biggest I'm-a-totally-normal-person-who-knows-how-to-eat-salad-dressing smile and she slowly backed away.

And then I ate it. It was really hard. And I cried. And we laughed. And I think I worried the waitress when she came to refill our coffees (because of all the crying and the laughing). And as I have been so many times in our relationship, I was overcome with love and gratitude for Kirsten.

And now salad dressing is a little easier because since I've been home, I've been challenging it all by myself.

CHAPTER 61

Fear Foods List, Revised

Things I've struck out are things I can now eat or drink without incident, even if I don't find them easy. Some *are* easy now, but many are still a lot of work ... however, a strikethrough means that if someone were to put that thing in front of me, I could eat it.

~~Sweetened/milky coffee drinks (hot)~~
~~Sweetened milky coffee drink (cold)~~
Premade sandwich
~~Pasta~~
~~Croissant~~
~~Store-bought muffin, bran~~
~~Cakey muffin~~
~~Donut~~
~~Smoothie~~
~~Scone~~
~~Biscuit~~
~~Gelato~~
~~Ice cream sandwich~~
~~Restaurant breakfast food (French toast or pancakes)~~
~~Cookie (packaged with calorie count)~~

~~Ice cream cake~~
Wrap
~~Restaurant/food stand taco~~
~~Beavertail~~
~~Falafel (no sauce)~~
~~Cookie, not packaged, no calorie count~~
Cupcake
~~Cake~~
Cake with icing
Pastry
~~Cinnamon bun~~
~~Ice cream~~
Quiche
~~Things with melted cheese (not most pizza now though)~~
Brownie
Pie
Falafel (with sauce)
~~Store bought Mexican fast food (i.e., Chipotle, Whole Foods, Taco Bell)~~
Sushi with gross orange mayo slathered on it.
~~Premade salad with nuts, seeds, quinoa, chickpeas~~
~~Salad with dressing~~
Salad with dressing cheese/nuts
"Bowls" s/as
  – ~~Poke bowl~~
  – Burrito bowl
  – Noodle bowl
Breaded things
Fried fish
French fries
~~Thai noodle soup with spicy oil~~

All things that come in a sauce, including:
- Stir fry
- All Thai food
- All Chinese food
- All Indian food

Macaroni and cheese

Most Italian food (restaurant pasta, lasagna, etc.)

Movie popcorn

Poutine

I suppose this means I need to start working on the other things on this list, the ones I've been avoiding. A large part of me doesn't want to. I don't feel like I'm missing out. I can easily go the rest of my life without any of those things … and I've been working so hard, I want a break. But I can't be a person who is recovered, who eats everything except things with sauces, things with batter, and things that seem too oily, too sugary, or too calorically dense. That's not recovery.

Bloody hell.

CHAPTER 62

January 15, 2021

<u>To Do, 4.0</u>

- Practice bottom part of fear foods list
- Practice top part of fear foods list (don't let those things get hard again)
- Go through closet and get rid of things that will never fit again
- Stop thinking that maybe they will fit again
- Remember that they should never fit again
- Keep practicing days of no-walking until they feel okay
- Stop worrying that you will never want to walk again and that you will end up a lazy slug
- Really think about whether you'd rather be trapped in an eating disorder forever or a lazy slug
- Look into whether slugs are actually lazy
- Think about all the things you can do now that used to feel impossible
- Stop thinking about all the things you still can't do, that still feel impossible
- Celebrate your victories

- Don't let your eating disorder convince you that they aren't victories
- Stop feeling so guilty all the time
- Embrace your bigger body and remember that it's a sign of healing
- Don't let your eating disorder convince you that you don't want to heal
- Turn that frown upside down, live, laugh, love, etc.

CHAPTER 63

The word "trigger" is one of my least favorite words (I also don't like "bosom," but for different reasons). Maybe it's because it's been adopted by people who are generally dramatic and whiny (remember when the day hospital mean girl was allegedly triggered when I mentioned *cat vomit*?) and maybe it's because I don't think that it should apply to me. I'm an adult woman who knows exactly what I'm supposed to be doing, and I like to think of myself as strong and not easily offended—I remember as a first-year undergrad proudly telling the middle-aged men I worked out with at the Y that they could tell *any* dirty joke they wanted. But the truth is that some dirty jokes are pretty offensive, and I'm not always strong. Sometimes people's words get to me.

This part of recovery, the part where I look okay and everyone thinks I'm fine, is the loneliest place to be. I'm generally too embarrassed to talk about how impossibly hard everything still feels, or how talk of a long-run-juice-fast-missed-breakfast-witty-peloton-instructor can send me spiraling.

Sure, juice fasts are boneheaded, and when someone talks about doing one, the first thing I do is re-evaluate how smart I might have thought that person was, but my next thought is always that I'm talking to a person who clearly cares about changing their body, or keeping their body small. And then, to my mind, that person is now representative of all humankind. Because obviously if this one person is doing a juice fast, it's evidence that *everyone* cares about changing their body or keeping their body small. And I'm clearly making a terrible mistake by allowing mine to get bigger.

I forget in the moment that what other people do has nothing to do with me or my body. I also forget that for most people, a diet won't change their life. They can do a three-day juice fast and then go back to living as usual. A diet won't swallow them whole.

I'm also sometimes triggered (ugh. Is there a synonym we can use? Set off? Provoked? Sparked?) by people who have active eating disorders. There are people close to me, some who know what I'm up to, and some who don't, who have very unhealthy relationships with exercise and food and have no intention of changing. And while you'd think I'd feel sad for them because I know exactly what that's like, sometimes their eating disorders seem happier and easier than my recovery and I long for the numb bliss of anosognosia.

Recently, my young daughters gave their very last mini donut (their favorite thing ever) to a family friend who'd come over for dinner. This was a huge honor and a show of love (my kids *really* don't like sharing) and she refused to taste it. I watched her awkwardly holding this tiny donut, having avoided the entire dinner, while they looked at her expectantly. She couldn't even take a bite of a *bite-sized* donut, and she asked me for a napkin to stash it in. And at that moment I was sad for my disappointed kids, and I was sad for her—I've been the person looking for a napkin to stash my mini-donut (cookie, chocolate, banquet meal) in more times than I care to admit. But after she went home, I couldn't stop thinking about my body compared to hers, and what she must think about what I'm doing. Does she think I've let myself go? Is she happier than I am? I used to be the thin one, and now, it's her. Does she think that I'm a failure?

To be clear, I'm not triggered by severely emaciated bodies. A couple of weeks ago, I had to block someone on the Instagram

Recovery account that I started in order to connect with other people in recovery. She was relentlessly sending me photos of her very ill body (she wasn't looking for help—she was looking to drag as many people down with her as possible). The sight of her photos was an anti-trigger for me—whenever I see someone who is that ill, I am overcome with gratitude not to be there anymore. I still don't quite understand how I was able to pull myself out of my last severe relapse the summer before my second year of undergrad, and I never want to go back to that place. This is not true for everyone. Anorexia can be a competitive illness, and some people aspire to look as ill as possible, even seeking out *pro-ana* sites—"thinspiration" websites designed by very ill people to be used by very ill people—to trigger *themselves*. I find this practice infuriating and depressing, but not triggering. For me personally, it's being around real, happy—or happy-seeming—people who can do the things I currently can't, namely engage in exercise and dieting, that makes me doubt everything I'm doing.

I don't really compare myself to people around me, except when it comes to food restriction and exercise. There is a very good chance that your house is less dusty than mine. I can guarantee your closet is cleaner, unless you are an actual hoarder. I don't feel extreme guilt when I hear about other people's cleaning binges, or hobbies (especially when their hobby is cleaning). I have a friend who sews beautifully, and while I'm impressed by her accomplishments, I don't feel bad for having to take loose buttons to the tailor (someone has to keep them in business). I don't feel bad about myself when I hear about other people taking courses or raising chickens, or plastering things (don't ask me what, I tune out for these conversations), but if you tell me a story about your Peloton instructor I might smile and make it through the rest of the conversation, but I'm not really listening anymore. I'm drowning in a sea of guilt, and I'm trying to remind myself that just because you work out, doesn't mean that I'm making a terrible, regrettable mistake.

But here's the thing—I have to learn to live in the world. Just because I'm recovering, it doesn't mean that diet culture will cease to exist. Recovery from an eating disorder is counter to many of the messages we receive from the media and our friends and strangers, and that's not going to change any time soon. So that leaves the changing up to me. I need to get better at remembering my reasons.

Not that long ago I was at a writing workshop and the facilitator mentioned she's a runner and that there is an adage among runners that it's important to get out every day, even if it's only for a couple of miles. That some running is always better than none.

I stopped listening as my thoughts got louder and louder. Why can't I run? She runs every day. I'm so lazy. I should really start running again. Though (much) later that evening it crossed my mind that her every day is probably not every. single. day. Her couple of miles is probably a *couple* of miles. She's probably able to take days off for vacations, and illness, and because she's busy, and because she doesn't feel like it. She can probably stop when she's tired. And if she can't, that's not the life I want.

I thought about what my life was like when I ran or exercised every day. Through illness, and injuries, and storms, and scalding heat and windchill warnings. Through labor pains and study sessions. On exam days and wedding days and holidays. It was never just a couple of miles. It was never enough.

I spent most of my life believing that getting out every day was better than not getting out. That wasn't true for me. I decided carefully and purposefully that I don't want that for myself anymore.

It's so hard not to compare. And it's so easy to doubt what I'm doing when it feels like the entire universe is pulling me in the opposite direction. But health is relative. Maybe, for some people, running every single day is healthy. I'm not them. And what they do has nothing to do with my recovery.

I guess the point is that I can't compare myself to people who aren't doing what I'm doing. I can't compare myself to someone with a healthy relationship with exercise, or even an unhealthy one. In those moments, I have to remember that comparing my food and exercise to someone else's is no different than comparing myself to their DIY-home improvement projects. What's good for them is not necessarily good for me (or my home). I have to remember why I'm doing this. I have to remember that I value being able to accept a donut from children who love me, more than I value a small body.

CHAPTER 64

Yesterday I put on jeans and was shocked when they fit. To my mind I had become so fat that there was no way I could possibly squeeze into them.

I don't really have much of an idea what my body looks like. I could pick myself out of a police line-up, but if you gave me a bunch of different photoshopped versions of my own body—some fatter, some thinner, I'd have trouble choosing which one was mine (but I think it's probably fair to say that I wouldn't be veering in the direction of any of the thinner options).

When I was at my most ill, I remember my psychiatrist-neighbor-family-friend telling me he was shocked by how thin I was when he saw me from the side. And I remember saying *"yeah, I know."* But I didn't know. I actually had no idea. I understood that I was very underweight, but I didn't see it. I didn't see a difference at that weight any more than I did when I was ten pounds heavier than that, the fall of my second year of undergrad when I was approached by the head of residence to discuss my anorexia (is she *kidding me*? I'm fine!) or ten pounds heavier than that, and a mother of three in the midst of an accidental mini relapse (why can't my pants stay up? what the actual hell?). To me, I always just look like … me.

When I was fifteen or sixteen a man in the hazy, opaque-aired smoking area of the cafeteria at the children's hospital (likely the dad of a child being treated for something… no one chose to hang out there) asked me and my friend, another inpatient, why such pretty girls would choose to starve ourselves. I wasn't so much flabbergasted by the rudeness of a strange adult man coming up to us and asking such a thing, as I was by the fact he had somehow known why we were in there. How did he know?

At the time, the hospital's practice was to take photos of us on admission in our underwear for our files (and no amount of protestation could change that). This was so obviously degrading I feel like I don't need to explain why, but every once in a while I wonder about those photos. What would I make of them now?

I sometimes come across photos taken a few years ago, in the midst of my accidental mini relapse, and I can see scrawny arms and legs and bony shoulders. Though when I was in it, I didn't see it, even in those same photos. This is why it took me so long to notice. I got used to each number on the scale before seeing a lower one, so when I finally saw the number that startled me, it was because it was familiar—the slipperiest part of a slippery slope. For months prior to that, I knew nothing fit anymore, that I had to roll up my pants at the waist several times to keep them up, and that there was no size of jeans in any adult store that I could wear without multiple adjustments, but I didn't see it in the mirror. Though I do remember asking a friend, who had remarked on it, if my thinness was unattractive. Had this friend—who worships at the altar of very thin bodies—said yes, I might have gone for help sooner.

I'm more comfortable at a lower weight (well *duh*, please see book jacket). What I mean by that is because I can't tell what my body looks like, and because of how my body is used to feeling, I panic when things feel different. For all the years until this recovery effort, as long as I fit into X-size jeans and never weighed over X-pounds and had X-much room between my thighs, I was okay. And now I don't fit into X-size jeans, and I weigh more than I ever have, and the shape of my thighs is completely different from what I'm used to.

And I have no idea what I look like. Sometimes I suspect I'm not as big as I think (usually when I can wear a piece of clothing that I was certain would no longer fit) but mostly, I trust what I see.

One way I've managed throughout my life has been by body checking—picture someone who is hearing impaired who learns to read lips. I would stand every day in front of my mirror and check the space between my thighs, and then stand sideways and examine my stomach in relation to my hip bones. But in recovery, those body parts are changing too, and I don't know how to reconcile any of it—imagine being that same person now trying to hear someone who is wearing a mask over their mouth. I don't know how my recovered thighs are supposed to look. Logically I understand that they have to look different, but I have one or two issues around logic when I'm looking in the mirror.

I've heard from recovered people that this changes. That a lot of the way we look at ourselves evolves as our bodies heal and brain volume returns to normal (oh yeah, if you are contemplating anorexia, you should probably know you will lose brain volume along with stubborn inches around your waist). Studies show that brain volume is completely restored with adequate weight gain and time—though it would be really nice if the regions of the brain affecting cognitive function as it applies to food, exercise, body image could be restored before having to go through the drudgery of weight gain (is there a letter I can send someone to fix this?).

So what's the solution? The truth is that I have no idea.

I take slight consolation in the fact that a lot of people have issues around self-perception (everyone who's been hit on by an overconfident gym bro at some point can confirm this). Some of us are aware of them, and some of us aren't.

I think learning to find things I value about myself beyond the size of my body is the only real way to deal with this. That and knowing it doesn't really matter if I look exactly like what I see in the mirror, or if I don't. Maybe that's the whole point.

CHAPTER 65

One morning last week, my almost-teenage son was yelling at me to help him find something before leaving for school, "Mom!" "Mom!" "Mom!" "MOOOOOOOM." I was in my bathroom, drying my hair in my bra and underwear. Exasperated, I ran downstairs (passing my husband who was standing. right. there.), handed my son the thing he was looking for—apparently invisible to everyone but me—and headed back up the stairs.

"Mommy?" I stop, wondering if this is the day I've only heard about and seen in TV movies—the day he actually thanks me for something. I turn to face him.

"Mommy, you are gaining weight. Sorry if this sounds rude, but you are."

I quickly walk up the rest of the stairs.

DON'TCRYDONTCRYDONTCRYDONTCRYDON'T CRYDONTCRYDONTCRYDONTCRY

I finish drying my hair, get dressed, and walk my youngest to school.

DONTCRYDONTCRYDONTCRYDONTCRYDON'T CRYDONTCRYDONTCRYDONTCRY

I smile at people at school drop-off and bump into a friend and talk and laugh for a minute and then walk in the opposite direction of her house, and mine.

DONTCRYDONTCRYDONTCRYDONTCRYDON'T
CRYDONTCRYDONTCRYDONTCRY

I want to run as fast and long as I can, until I can't feel the hurt and the shame, but as I'm in winter boots and a parka and have a call with Emily in just over an hour, I settle on an illicit walk.

This kid doesn't notice anything. Our house could be painted an entirely different color tomorrow, and there is only a fifty percent chance he'd notice. Our cat could go missing, and he wouldn't notice. I could replace one of his sisters with a stunt double, and he wouldn't notice.

But he noticed that my body has changed.

I text Kirsten, and she initially thinks it's funny (we don't always have the same sense of humor, I've also stopped sending her TikToks). Then she realizes how upset I am.

She reminds me that the body he is used to seeing isn't a healthy one, and that a sick, starving body shouldn't be his standard of female attractiveness. She tells me that I'm doing a service to his future partners (and I can't help but wonder about all of the ways in which I've already failed those same partners. I don't think he's ever hung up a jacket, or made his bed, except under duress).

Cali says mostly the same things but without using the words *heteronormative assumptions*.

They are both really kind, and say smart, insightful things. But I need someone to feel sad with me. I want someone to acknowledge how much this hurts.

I tell Emily about it on our call, and she blames me for not having told him what I'm doing. I try to explain to her that he's twelve and wouldn't understand, and that he would tell everyone about this thing he doesn't understand. She tells me that it's my job to help him understand.

Her frustration is palpable. *Of course* my body is changing, that's the point. If it wasn't, nothing else could be changing. And *of course* my kid is going to notice, and if I don't tell him what's going on, well that's on me. And if I'm ashamed to tell people about why I'm gaining weight, that's also on me. I am *supposed to be* gaining weight. I can't gain all the life things without gaining weight. Why can't I understand that?

I get it. Isn't it better for my children to have a mother who can teach them that it's possible to overcome seemingly insurmountable obstacles than a mother who fits into the tiniest size of pants?

Isn't it more important to have a mother who can model healthy, balanced attitudes around food and exercise than one who acts like exercise is more important than all other things?

Isn't it more important to have a mother who is present, who can go for spontaneous ice cream, and who can happily stay in all day and watch movies on the couch, than it is to have a mother whose body never changes?

Then why didn't my kid say he notices that I eat dinner with him now? Or that we no longer have to walk absolutely everywhere? Or that because I'm no longer exercising at crazy o'clock every morning I'm now joining him downstairs for breakfast?

Maybe the extra weight is the only thing that he can see.

I'd like to think that recovery is making me more available, more open, more empathetic, more honest, less afraid, less rigid.

But right now, I feel more distracted, more self-conscious, more anxious, more self-critical and more alone than I've ever felt.

It doesn't feel worth it.

Does my son really care about the way my body looks? Maybe he only mentioned I was gaining weight because he was so excited that he finally noticed something. But his words really hurt me. I'm still getting used to my changing body, and this was a stark reminder that other people can see the changes too. And I don't know if I'm ready for that.

CHAPTER 66

Monday

7:00 a.m. Draft an email to Emily telling her I want to skip our next session because I'm feeling terrible about my body, and I need time to think about everything. Put it in my drafts folder.

11:00 a.m. Reread it. Put it back in my drafts folder.

11:15 a.m. Reread it. Put it back in my drafts folder.

11:55 a.m. Reread it. Put it back in my drafts folder.

12:05: p.m. Reread it. Put it back in my drafts folder.

12:20 p.m. Ask my husband if he thinks it's rude if I cancel my appointment with Emily for the following day. He doesn't ask why, but says it's definitely fine given I've never canceled or missed a session in all our time together. I want him to ask why I'm canceling. I hold back tears.

1:05 p.m. Reread the email. Put it back in my drafts folder.

1:30 p.m. Send the email. Relief. I'm done. I go for a proscribed walk.

3:00 p.m. I hear back from Emily, it's a really nice email. She says I shouldn't be *retreating into my pain* and that we should meet.

I don't know if she knows I'm seriously contemplating quitting. I'm torn. I draft a response but don't send it. I keep walking until it's time to pick up my youngest from school.

6:00 p.m. Dinner. I don't have what my family is eating, opting instead for my pre-recovery default meal of tofu and steamed broccoli. It's vile. How did I eat this every day? Can I get used to it again? Do I want to?

8:00 p.m. Chair a committee meeting for my kids' school's parent council while trying to keep attendees from falling asleep. I'm a little hungry by the time it's over, probably as a result of having undereaten all day, and because my body has gotten used to being fed. *Ugh. Annoying.*

10:30 p.m. Have a snack, rationalizing that there's room in my calorie allotment. Immediately feel guilty about it.

10:45 p.m. Reread Emily's email. I have to get back to her, I just don't know what to say.

11:55 p.m. Write Emily back. Tell her I'd like to cancel. Get teary after I hit send. Can't figure out why I'm so sad.

3:00 a.m. Wake up thinking about the fastest way to get back to a body I recognize. Fantasize about restriction and exercise and weight loss.

3:30 a.m. Start planning the fastest way to get back to a body I recognize. Make plans to restrict and exercise and lose weight.

3:55 a.m. Get a little scared. Feel like my brain has been fully hijacked. Send Emily an email asking if we can meet if she's still free.

4:15 a.m. Regret sending the email.

Tuesday

9:00–10:20 a.m. Go for a fast walk after school drop off. I'm done. I'm done. I'm done. I don't have to pretend anymore.

10:30 a.m. Meet with Emily. Tell her that I think that I'm done with recovery. Expect her to try to talk me out of it. She doesn't. She tells me to take the week to think about it but in the meantime to try to keep our current rules in place, if I can.

11:45 a.m. Grab a quick lunch before running out the door for a massage appointment. Don't care that it's not a recovery-appropriate lunch. I'm done with recovery. Phew.

12:10 p.m. Massage. Listen to my massage therapist make her usual comments about how small I am and how big she is compared to me. They bother me a tiny smidge less than usual. I mutter my customary lines about how she looks great the way she is (and mean them).

1:15 p.m. Go for a walk. Tell myself I can do whatever I want.

3:12 p.m. Arrive home just in time to leave for school pickup. Have a moment of regret for having wasted my entire afternoon walking, and then console myself with a reminder that I finished my audio book. Time spent reading is never wasted, and I was basically reading.

4:00 p.m. Go skating with my daughter. I congratulate myself on my no-more-recovery plan because of how laid back I feel about skating, given all the walking I've already done. My life is better already!

5:30 p.m. Walk to pick up my youngest from a playdate. I'm afraid to look at my step count, knowing it's going to be absurdly high. Don't want to feel like I have to match it tomorrow.

6:15 p.m. Dinner. I'm really hungry, having had a pretty small lunch and breakfast. Wonder if I'll lose my hunger cues again and if that's something I want. Can't decide if I'm stopping here (done challenging things), or if I'm jumping back into active restriction. I'm very careful with my dinner portion, just in case.

7:20 p.m. Kirsten texts. Asks how I'm doing. I haven't told her (or anyone) about any of this. I contemplate telling her, but decide against it, suspecting that it will just annoy her. I ignore her question and ask her to send me photos of her new puppy. It's the distraction we all need. That dog is adorable, especially in a giant handbag.

8:30 p.m. Friends come by for backyard drinks. I contemplate having wine but decide to stick to tea, like a couple of my friends. It's cold out and we are outside, and in addition to not being as warm as tea, wine doesn't feel worth the calories.

9:45 p.m. The subject turns to exercise. One of my friends mentions that she and her husband work out every single day in their home gym. I panic a little and then remember all the walking I did. *It's okay, I'm okay.*

11:50 p.m. Get ready for bed. Look in my full-length mirror. Feel less fat already. Take a moment to ponder how nonsensical that is.

4:00 a.m. My stomach growls. Wonder if I'm making a terrible mistake.

Wednesday

6:30 a.m. Check my email for something from Emily. She always emails a summary the day after a session. Nothing. Worry that she's angry or disappointed. Remind myself that it's my life and who cares what she thinks (me, I care. I really hate that I've disappointed her).

Remind myself that I can't recover because I'm worried about disappointing Emily. Think about how disappointed some of my close friends will be too. Distract myself with the Wordle. I do extremely well. Who needs recovery? I'm really, really great at anticipating and rearranging letters.

7:00 a.m. Use artificial sweetener in my oatmeal. Was it always this cloying?

9:00 a.m. Go for a quick walk after school drop-off, making sure to arrive home on time for an online appointment with my son. Am stressed about stopping my walk (and about being on camera with my outspoken twelve-year-old at an appointment I'm forcing him to attend).

11:45 a.m. Lunch. Have egg whites always tasted this … watery?

12:10 p.m. Leave for a walk. Tell myself I won't waste my entire afternoon again, that I'll stop earlier this time.

2:55 p.m. Arrive home. Realize I've wasted my entire afternoon. Again.

3:20 p.m. Walk to pick up my youngest from school.

6:00 p.m. Dinner, I carefully measure my pasta when no one is looking. Freedom is mine! (Or is it?)

8:30 p.m. Kirsten sends a really sweet article about friendship. Again, I contemplate telling her what's going on. Decide against it. What's the point?

10:30 p.m. Have a snack. I'm still hungry. Debate whether to have something else. Decide not to.

10:35 p.m. Start filling out my HabitShare app for Emily. Too many red circles (denoting failed agreements around meals and exercise).

I delete the day's entries. Besides, what does she care? She hasn't even emailed me. I'm clearly dead to her.

11:50 p.m. Get ready for bed. Avoid looking at my body.

4:00 a.m. Wake up hungry. Seriously, body?

Thursday

6:30 a.m. Check for an email from Emily. Nothing. Decide I don't care if she doesn't care (but I do).

9:00 a.m. After school drop-off, walk in the direction of home with a friend who lives nearby. When we part ways, make sure that I'm out of eyeshot, and head back in the direction of the school to go for a walk. Wonder why I couldn't admit I was going for a walk—this friend doesn't even know about my recovery. It's not like I'm going to deal illegal drugs or shoplift or even browse in the tacky sex store in my neighborhood. Why do I feel like a criminal?

10:00 a.m. Walk toward home. I have a walk scheduled with my friend in the evening and a very long to-do list, and I can't waste another day walking. Draft a post for my Insta recovery account. I often draft things to sound a little more pro-recovery than I feel, but I reflect on this one. Maybe I do want to recover.

10:20 a.m. I have a snack.

11:35 a.m. Reread my Insta post. Decide to leave it in drafts for now.

12:00 p.m. Make lunch. Use real eggs in my omelette but avoid greasing the pan. They stick. Decide to have toast with the eggs, and use margarine, thinking about how hard I've worked to be able to do that.

2:00 p.m. I'm itching to go for a walk. Do yoga instead. Changing out of jeans into leggings and back into jeans is as much effort as the actual yoga, but I feel pretty good about my healthy distraction technique.

3:15 a.m. Walk to school pickup. A friend asks me and my daughter to go skating, and although it's unlike me to ever turn down any kind of exercise, ever (even fake exercise like skating), I ask for a rain check. I'm tired and cold and a lot less happy than I should be, given that I've finally broken up with stupid, annoying recovery.

6:00 p.m. Dinner. For the second time since Monday, I don't eat with my family, once again opting for good old steamed broccoli and tofu. For the second time since Monday, the smell almost makes me gag.

8:20 p.m. Meet a friend for a walk. It's a snowstorm. She's the first person I tell that I think I've maybe, probably, possibly quit recovery. She tells me I always relapse in February, and that it's just a blip, and that it will all work out (but in the nicest way possible).

Friday

6:30 a.m. Wake up to a text message from Emily asking me to update our HabitShare app. Now she cares? I ignore the text.

7:00 a.m. Breakfast. Opt for sugar in my oatmeal.

9:00 a.m. Meet Cali for a longish walk after school drop-off. Tell her everything but somehow manage to make the story pretty funny. We laugh hard, and then she tells me I need to get back to Emily. I tell her I'll think about it.

12:00 p.m. Lunch. Won't get me a green circle on HabitShare, but I wouldn't be ashamed to enter it.

12:20 p.m. My brother calls to ask me a legal question about his calorie counting app. It's again very apparent he thinks that he is doing good—saving people from sneaky hidden calories and the terrible fate of not burning as much as they eat. I wonder for the eleventy-billionth time if he has any idea what I'm going through, or if he's ever wondered. I give him mediocre advice and feel okay about it.

12:30–3:15 p.m. Manage to stay home all afternoon despite an extreme urge to walk. Maybe I can stop here—in this place of not that sick but not that well—and be fine.

4:00 p.m. Write Emily back. Tell her I'll fill out the HabitShare to make her happy, but that I don't feel like I should have to during this, my Super Special Recovery Vacation/Contemplation Week.

4:05 p.m. She writes back to say that regardless of whether I'm bailing or on the fence, that she needs to know the details of what I'm doing.

4:45 p.m. Walk my daughter and her friends to a dance class and have forty-five minutes to kill. Contemplate another walk, but instead go find my friend who has texted to say she's in a nearby coffee shop waiting for her daughter to finish the same class. Another friend joins us, and I'm happy to be there and not out in the cold walking aimlessly.

6:00 p.m. Dinner. I'm anxious about a meal I've had hundreds of times since starting recovery, not so much the contents, but how much to eat. It's all become complicated very quickly.

6:25 p.m. I write Emily back to say I don't think that I'm bailing.

6:26 p.m. She replies immediately: "Excellent."

CHAPTER 67

Reasons to keep going (in no particular order)

1. I won't spend the rest of my life wondering *what-if?*
2. I've already invested so much time and energy (and money! All this coaching adds up!).
3. I won't disappoint the people who care about me.
4. This might actually work out if I keep going—it definitely won't if I stop.
5. I can always stop later. I'm not signing a pledge in blood.
6. If I stop now, Emily might not take me back if I want to start again later.
7. I'm setting a better example for my children in every possible way.
8. If I stop, things won't stay static. I'll slip back (last week made that very apparent. How many more nights do I want to spend eating tofu for dinner and walking alone in the dark and cold?)
9. Better book ending.
10. Not letting the ED win (this should be persuasive enough on its own).
11. Better for my bones and overall health.
12. Living by my values (I don't care at all about what other people's bodies look like, why is mine so important? Why am I such a hypocrite? Hypocrites are the actual worst).

13. If I stop here, I'll never be able to enjoy a day of rest or a meal that someone else made, or even a mixed drink (of the non-gin and soda variety) without stress.
14. I will never learn that I have value beyond my body.
15. I really do believe that full recovery is possible for other people. I am not a unicorn.

Reasons to Stop

1. It's so exhausting and time-consuming and I'm tired of being sad and anxious and stressed out all the time. (*I will probably be just as sad if I give up and slip back into walking countless hours a day and only being able to eat five foods, I know too much now, denial isn't an option anymore.*)
2. I can feel more confident in my body. (*Oh crap. Wait. Isn't confidence supposed to come from within? Fuckity fuck.*)
3. I can fit back into all my old cute clothes. (*I can buy new clothes!*)
4. I won't feel like a weirdo or an alien when other people talk about exercise. (*I will always be a weirdo if I don't get my addiction under control, even if on the outside everything looks normal.*)
5. I will be less distracted. (*Except I will always have an ED chattering away in the background.*)
6. What if I end up failing and waste two more years? I can save myself the anguish. (*Okay, this is idiotic. Why start anything? Nothing is guaranteed.*)
7. I don't believe it's going to work. (*Yes. I do! That's why I started this in the first place. I believe in full recovery.*)
8. What if I recover and everyone thinks I'm fat and let myself go? (*This is the dumbest one yet. Why do I care so much about what other people think? Is *this* a reason not to recover?*)
9. I'm so scared.

CHAPTER 68

When I was a teenager with anorexia, social media didn't exist (because the internet didn't exist, because I was basically a minor character on *The Flintstones*). This was good in many ways. I wasn't comparing myself to filtered people who don't even look like *themselves* let alone real humans. I didn't have to deal with the pressure of making sure I had enough Instagram followers, or Facebook friends, or likes, or shares, or loves, or smiley faces. And the only kind of ads I was exposed to were the ones in magazines, which didn't really phase me (I am not someone who thinks the fashion industry or Barbie can give someone an eating disorder).

Still, I didn't know anyone else who was going through the same things I was. It would have been nice to have felt like part of a community of people trying to get better, or to know that such people existed. Maybe I would have gotten better thirty years ago (this is hard to contemplate for too long).

I so desperately wanted to find other people who had anorexia that I read the same memoirs over and over—always written by adult women who weren't well—and any article about eating disorders I could get my hands on (in secret, in the library. I'm sure anyone watching my behavior presumed I was looking at back-issues of *Playgirl*, not articles about Karen Carpenter).

There was a TV movie that came out when I was about thirteen that I recorded and watched over and over and over and over. It's about a woman who is bulimic and passes out at an exercise class and is immediately hospitalized for her eating disorder. Her roommate has anorexia and they go through treatment together and Ed Asner plays the insightful, caring but stern doctor. That was all I yearned for: a roommate who wanted to get better with me and Ed Asner to fix us in group therapy (I should probably add that the anorexic roommate dies, but otherwise that movie represented everything I thought I needed).

But once I was hospitalized, even though I did meet other people with anorexia, some of whom I liked a great deal, there was no group therapy or talk of getting better. The hospital was an echo chamber. We were teenagers on a medical unit being forced to gain weight against our will. We weren't trying to get better, we were trying to stay off bed rest. We were trying to avoid tube feeding. We were trying to stay safe—and ill.

I think I would have benefited greatly from Recovery Instagram as a teen. For starters, I would have heard the word "recovery," a concept that never came up in all my hospitalizations. The closest I ever got to that concept was when my neighbor/psychiatrist/family friend made my mother buy me a black Nike T-shirt with "*Just Do It*" emblazoned on the front in hot pink cursive ("*I don't know what Andrew is thinking Sheri, I had to drive to three different stores and this T-shirt cost THIRTY-FIVE-DOLLARS*"). Unfortunately, no one told me what I was supposed to be "just doing."

It was just over a year ago that I started my Instagram recovery account, for the purpose of following other recovery accounts without anyone from my real life noticing (what would people think if they knew that I was still struggling? Or that I'd struggled? Or that I was trying to recover?). And then I decided to post, really so that the people I followed wouldn't think I was a weird creeper. And the more I posted, the more comfortable I became posting, and interacting with people. And eventually, even though that account was borne out of shame and secrecy, it made me feel less ashamed. I added a profile picture about nine months after my first post, and I added my first name about two months after that. I felt dizzy and shaky, and I thought I might cry and throw up when I added that photo, but today, I know that it was the right decision. Less secrecy and more openness have paid off once again. Who knew?!

I've met more fully recovered people on Instagram than I previously knew existed. I've met people who are fighting hard for their recovery. People who have been ill as long as I have. People who are young enough to be my children but who are full of hope and insight. I've learned brand new terms, and that things I thought were unique to me are actually symptoms of my illness. I've learned about neural rewiring and *Health at Every Size*. I've met some amazing people who are fighting for themselves and their lives, and some who are bottomless pits who will never get well, and who want to drag everyone down with them.

My extremely profound and original point is that social media can be very helpful, or very unhelpful, and like with anything else, you are the boss of that.

In that spirit, I've decided to compile a list of tips. As always, my advice is worth exactly what you paid for it (presuming you bought this book on a discount rack or shoplifted it). I'm only on Instagram, but I know that there are a lot of recovery accounts on TikTok too. I suspect most of the same rules apply.

1. Be careful about who you follow. People who post photos of their ill bodies or who want to talk about their lowest weights or hospitalizations are not trying to get better. They are trying to prove something. Stay away.

2. *What I Eat in a Day* posts can be very triggering if you are someone prone to comparison. Maybe you want to see what normal looks like, but no one posting everything they eat on the internet is normal. Stay away.

3. You don't have to follow people back and you can unfollow them indiscriminately. Worst case scenario, they unfollow you too. Who cares? Seriously.

4. If you are posting, always write with the sickest person following you in mind. Don't use numbers. Don't talk about restriction. Don't talk about over-exercise. This isn't confession or therapy or your diary. Don't be a selfish dolt.

5. You don't have to respond to every DM or give anyone your life story. Be discerning. If someone is harassing you, block them.

6. There are a LOT of very young people on social media. Sometimes it will feel like high school. You don't have to engage any more than you want to (even if you are in high school).

7. Don't go on Recovery Insta trying to get famous.

8. There are some very popular accounts that are truly wonderful.

9. There are some very popular accounts that are truly terrible.

10. There are some very popular accounts run by truly terrible people. Be careful.

11. If someone talks about recovery all the time but looks emaciated, it's not because they are naturally skinny, I promise.

12. If someone's recovery journey turns into a health and fitness journey, they aren't recovered. Their illness has simply shape-shifted. Unfollow.

13. If it's stressing you out, take a break. I post at most once a week and sometimes take weeks off at a time. For me that feels like enough.

14. Be kind but don't jeopardize your own recovery. Oxygen masks, blah, blah, blah.

15. Trust your gut. I've made a few amazing friends on Instagram. They have always been respectful and kind. If something doesn't feel right, end it.

16. You don't know what's true, or what isn't. Instagram is a filtered snapshot of people's lives. Don't compare your progress to a set of slides.

17. Similarly, don't compare your struggles to other people's. You are sick enough to recover. Your recovery is valid.

18. Take your own advice. It's easy to get into the habit of proselytizing all the things you know to be true and never acting on them. What's the point of that?

19. Don't copy other people's posts. That's so tacky.

20. Check your spelling.

CHAPTER 69

I was chubby in grade four, and five, and part of grade six. According to my doctor, and my parents, the difference between where I was (not as cute as I should be) and where I could be (filling all of my cute-potential) was about ten pounds. Which I guess is meaningful for someone who is child-sized? I mean, I have kids but don't ask me how tall any of them are, I only know that they are shorter than me.

Here's the thing: I didn't notice. I heard it talked about all the time, but still chose ice cream and chips and chocolate and cream soda over thinness. I took "such a shame, you have such a pretty face" as "you have a pretty face!" I took "you only look fat from the front and not the back" as a comment that my mom appreciated my thinner back, and I never once thought about entering a room backward. Even the summer going into grade five, when a friend made a comment that I looked a little fatter every time she saw me (I think that probably had more to do with my affinity for tight T-shirts and short-shorts than actual body changes between spring and summer) it didn't sting in the way I feel like it should have, and the way it stings now. Most importantly, it didn't shake me out of my stupid, fat, happy state.

I was blissfully ignorant, until I wasn't. And for most of my life I've looked back at those years between grade four and the winter of grade six—the winter of my life-changing epiphany (can "epiphany" be used to describe the spark that ignited decades of illness?) with so much shame. How could I not have cared or noticed? Why didn't I fix it sooner? And wrapped up in that shame, there has also been the promise to my young self that I'd never let it happen again. Instead of being mad at the adults around me for not protecting me, or at least accepting me (that one comment from my friend was the only one made by a child) for making me feel less-than, for erasing any sense of pride or accomplishment or self-worth I might have had looking back at those years, I've been so mad at myself for having been so fat and stupid and overconfident. How dare I have been happy? Running around in a bathing suit like I had nothing to be ashamed of? Why didn't I see it?

I'm so conflicted, because along with all that shame, I'm also heartbroken that I look back at years of illness and obsession as the elixir to that embarrassing larva version of my thin self. On the one hand, I'm so relieved that by the end of grade six I was slim and pretty and not-deluded. And on the other hand, I'm so sad for that girl in grade six, given what was to come. I have lived for so long with the narrative that my illness saved me, when in reality, it almost broke me. And not only in the metaphorical sense; it almost killed me, and even then, it felt like the best and only option. Even in hindsight. Even now, sometimes.

When people talk about full recovery being this thing where you accept yourself at any size, and you don't care because you are happy, I'm frightened. Because what if I'm happy, but I don't deserve to be? What if my friends think I'm a little fatter every time they see me? Then what? I'm having so much trouble separating my feelings—this unshakable sense that the child-version of me was an embarrassment to be erased—from the truth: I was a little kid, I was okay.

Not everyone is going to like me (for starters, I'm unable to control vigorous eye rolling around people I find annoying; I talk a lot; I can be very sensitive; and I'm opinionated), but at least I know that people aren't judging me because of my body. Do I want to add one extra thing for people to potentially criticize? But do the people who matter really care if I get fat? And is this a reason not to recover? What would I tell my children or a friend in the same position? Do I like anyone more or less because of the way their body looks? *Of course I don't.* The truth is that I care so little about my friends' bodies, that in many cases I can't even picture what they look like from the neck down.

My children are around the same age I was when I first got sick, and I think about how hard I work to instil feelings of self-love and unconditional confidence in them. But I'm mortified to admit that I've always been slightly relieved that they are thin. Not because it affects the way I see them, but because I know that it's easier to be a thin child. Weight is the number one thing children are bullied for, and I never want them to be bullied or made to feel anything less than perfect the way they are. That said, I know—and believe with my whole heart—that they would be perfect at any size, and I understand that my most important job is making sure they know that too.

As I look back at that version of me, the before-version, I need to find and hold onto the good things—she was smart and creative and funny and social and loved her friends and family and would have been just fine if she'd never lost those ten pounds. I was lovable, even chubby, in tight T-shirts and short-shorts (also, why did my mother micromanage my weight but not my clothing?).

I have to separate my feelings about what happened in those years from what actually happened. Anorexia didn't save me.

CHAPTER 70

Today I used my fear of fries as a metaphor for recovery in a conversation with Emily. I described how even when I know I'm supposed to be challenging fries, after the first two or three, it gets really noisy, and I can't eat any more. I start thinking about how unnecessary they are, and how they can't possibly change anything, and how well I've done all of these years without fries. And how I was never really sure that I wanted fries anyway.

Emily chooses to take this literally and suggests that I should eat fries every day for a week.

My first instinct is to say no. Then I remember that I can't keep saying no. It's been a hard and demoralizing few weeks, and I know, and Emily knows, that if I keep saying no, nothing will change, and I'll get discouraged, and I'll quit. I need to say yes. I need a victory. I need to keep proving to myself that I can break ED rules, even the ones that have been firmly in place for most of my life.

So I say yes. I will have fries every day for a week.

And although I don't sign an agreement in blood (or even say all of this out loud), the rules are pretty clear: I can't have fries instead of a meal; they can be the smallest size, but I have to finish them; and I can't compensate later by making another meal smaller—all other rules around meals still stand.

Day 1

I go get fries as soon as I get off my call with Emily, before I lose my nerve. As it turns out, there is a McDonald's three hundred meters from my house (I knew it was close but having never been there, I didn't realize quite how close). I bring the fries home and plate them, ignoring the very strong urge to weigh them to make sure that McDonald's hasn't given me too large a serving. I make the rest of my lunch (omelette, sliced apple) and eat the other components first. Why the actual hell did I agree to this? Who eats fries with lunch anyway? *Fuckity fuck fuck fuck.* I'm sure they gave me too many. Realize the fries are now ice cold. Yuck. Maybe ketchup? Go get the ketchup from the fridge, trying to ignore the fact that ketchup is going to add more calories to what is already a calorie-dense meal. Ketchup helps. Feel like the fries are multiplying. Resist the urge to Google "How frequently does McDonald's give out too many fries?" and "What to do when McDonald's gives you too many fries?"

Finish the fries.

OMG.

Day one is done

Day 2

Go back to the same McDonald's and am relieved when it's someone new taking the orders. I don't want to be a regular quite yet. The woman who takes my order asks if I collect points and hands me a little card telling me about their app. Maybe she *did* see me yesterday? I tell her I'll look into the app (I do enjoy free stuff).

I'm already talking myself out of the fries on my short walk home. These are unnecessary. How on earth will *fries* even help me recover? What if I get addicted to fries and McDonald's (I'm sure

I saw a documentary about that)? Maybe I don't want to recover if it means eating stuff that I don't need or want and getting fat. I make myself some eggs and cut up another apple (this worked yesterday, so why not?) but I finish the eggs and the apple and still haven't taken the fries out of the (now greasy) bag. Deep breath. Open the bag, pour the fries onto a plate and remembering how much ketchup helped yesterday, go get some from the fridge. I hesitate because of the extra ketchup-calories and wonder if I should throw out three or four fries to make up for the ketchup but decide that's not in the spirit of this challenge and resist. I eat a fry. It's cold again. Like yesterday, they get exponentially harder as I eat. I Google "Calories in small McDonald's fries" even though I obviously know the answer and know that I shouldn't be Googling calories, rationalizing that it's okay to Google things I've already memorized (it's not okay. It's nuts. I know). I resist Googling "Sizing errors at McDonald's" and "How often do McDonald's employees give out too many fries?" and "There are too many fries in my bag, now what?" Finish the fries. Lots of guilt, but I'm done. Day two is done.

I sign up for the app.

Day 3

Head back into the same McDonald's after eating the first part of my lunch. I'm a little worried about judgment from the staff and am relieved that I'm not greeted like Norm from Cheers. I already know the price down to the penny before she tells me, but decide against pulling out my app.

Arrive home craving an apple. Pull the smaller greasy bag out of the larger greasy bag. I'm sure these fries are greasier than usual. Pour a blob of ketchup onto my plate. They definitely taste greasier. Resist the urge to blot them. Resist the urge to Google "Are McDonald's fries sometimes too greasy?" Resist the urge to throw them out.

Finish the fries. Feel simultaneously awful and triumphant (approximately a 70/30 split). Can't believe I have four days to go. Ugh.

Day 4

I am out running errands and decide to grab my fries at the McDonald's next to my dry cleaner to avoid the embarrassment of walking into the same McDonald's for the fourth day in a row. It's early, but as I always end up eating my fries cold anyway, I'm okay if they end up being a couple of hours old by the time lunch rolls around. I'm surprised by the number of people in line at McDonald's at 10:30 a.m. though. When it's my turn, I order. The cashier says "What?" I repeat myself. "It's breakfast" she says, speaking to me as if I'm an imbecile (or someone who has only been to McDonald's four times in thirty years). "Oh, sorry." I mutter and decide not to ask what time the fries begin.

I pass another McDonald's on my way home about half an hour later, and I stop there and order fries. They are serving them! The cashier asks if I have a points card. I use it!

I arrive home and pull out the McDonald's bag from the shopping bag filled with birthday presents for my cat. It's saturated with grease. Panic.

I can do this. I pull the fry bag out of the greasy brown McDonald's bag and it looks too full. I curse myself for being so friendly with the cashier—I bet she was trying to be nice, like that dastardly Whole Foods employee who smiled while telling me she was *intentionally* giving me the biggest piece of roasted salmon that time. Dammit.

I want to weigh the fries to see how far off they are from a regular serving. I plate them instead.

I eat three.

I go get my food scale. I weigh them. Then I weigh three on their own to make up for the three I just ate. As it turns out they are only nine grams heavier than the standard serving size (so still below the margin of error in my mental calorie allotment).

I sit down. I eat two more.

I go weigh them again. And then I weigh five on their own to make up for the five I ate.

Same weight. Huh. It seems like a lot more than that.

I feel guilty for weighing the fries. Regular people don't do that. And I have been so good about not weighing things lately. Though I'm relieved that the fries don't weigh as much as I expected, even though realistically nothing bad would happen to me if it had been twice as many fries for seven days in a row. But bad things will happen if I start weighing food regularly again.

I resume eating the fries and feel the guilt settling in before I've even reached the halfway point. In happy news, I'm more than halfway done the Week of Fries and I'm crushing it (except for accidentally weighing them twice today). I eat all of them, including the extra nine grams.

Day 5

Saturday. It's close to lunchtime and I find myself still in pyjamas, sorting baby clothes I'm giving to a pregnant friend. I tell my husband that I need to eat fries (knowing that he will understand that it's an agreement I've made with Emily, and that he won't have any follow-up questions), and I ask if he will run to McDonald's for me and get fries while I shower, aware that he loves McDonald's. He agrees, and I stress that they have to be a small. Not medium, not large, not extra-large, small S-M-A-L-L (he tends to tune out details when I'm speaking, obviously because of how interesting I am).

When he finally arrives home—he's decided to go by car to a drive-through fifteen minutes away, rather than walk to the one four minutes from our house—he hands me a large McDonald's bag containing what is either a large or a medium box of fries. They both come in a red box, so I'm not sure which size I've been handed, all I know is it's definitely not the small white bag I'm used to.

I tell him that it's the wrong size.

He insists that I'm wrong, and says it's absolutely a small, and when was the last time I even *saw* McDonald's fries?

Unable to believe that he is gaslighting (greaselighting?) me, I tell him that I've had a small fry every day for the past four days running and that is definitely not a small *thankyouverymuch*.

He says who cares and tells me to just eat the bigger one.

And then he rolls his eyes.

I storm upstairs. He does too. We only have one staircase. It's a bit awkward.

Even though I'm furious (and anxious and, well, really sad), I think about the fact that I've made a commitment to seven days of fries and know that I'll ultimately feel worse if I don't do it. So I eventually go back downstairs and pull out my trusty food scale, knowing full well that using my food scale two days in a row is definitely not okay and that this has to be the last time. But also, I can't eat the entire contents of that red box. (Note: on reread I guess it's obvious that I could have eaten the larger size, and that it probably would have been a great thing for my recovery, but I really didn't feel like I could.)

While I'm measuring out exactly seventy five grams (the weight of a small listed on the website, which I don't bother checking again) my youngest walks into the kitchen and asks what I'm doing. My heart drops. I've always worked really hard to hide disordered behaviors from my kids, and I feel like I've been caught doing something illegal. I tell her I'm seeing if McDonald's actually gives you as much as they say, because I read an article that some places don't (lying and covering up eating disorder behaviors is still my superpower, but I'm not proud—I feel like the Grinch lying about stealing presents to

Cindy Lou Who). I give my daughter the remaining fries and tell her to share them with her sister. She is thrilled.

I proceed to eat exactly seventy five grams of ice-cold fries. It goes pretty smoothly. I eat them at a normal pace, and I don't think about what I'm doing all that much. Maybe the secret is an argument with my husband every time I eat.

Day five is done.

Day 6

I order veggie burgers and fries for my family from a place we often order from (I usually get salad as my side). My husband goes to pick it up.

He calls me from the place to say their deep fryer is broken (*I'm sorry, what?*) and asks if we all want salad instead. I am so, so tempted to say yes, but instead—even though I'm next to my daughter—I say, "No. I need fries," like some kind of potato-addicted weirdo. She clearly finds this unremarkable (I guess she needs fries too). My husband begrudgingly agrees to stop at McDonald's on the way home to get us all fries. He's not thrilled about making the extra stop, but to my daughter, I'm a hero.

My husband arrives home. I'm getting pretty sick of McDonald's fries, so I'm less excited to see and smell them than the people in my household who haven't been eating them every day for the past week. I'm having an especially bad body-image day, so in addition to fry-ennui, there is a lot of ED noise, particularly because fries + burger is well above the number of calories I allow for any given meal, even though Emily and I have been working on raising that number incrementally for months.

I eat my burger and have some salad. My family has all finished eating before I turn my mind to my fries. Actually, that's a lie. My mind has been on the fries the whole time. My family has all finished eating by the time I've run out of all reasonable excuses not to have started eating the fries. I eat them alone, because everyone else has already wandered away.

I finish the fries.

Day 7

I'm trying to work out how I'm going to fit the fries into my day. I didn't eat fries at lunch because it was snowing, and I didn't feel like going out to get them (and also, I really, really didn't feel like eating them).

My husband is away, and I think about giving the kids veggie burgers and fries for dinner. Then I remember we did that last night. Ugh. Maybe omelettes and fries? Will that be precedent-setting? Can I deny that it ever happened, if they try to add it into our regular meal rotation? Or can we add that into our regular meal rotation? Maybe that's okay?

I ponder whether I should get McDonald's fries for everyone for the second day in a row or buy the frozen ones. If I buy the frozen ones, how do I figure out serving sizes? Oh my god. Why is this my life? I Google a brand of frozen fries that I've seen in commercials and look at how many come in a pack and decide that it wouldn't be unreasonable to split a regular bag four ways—that calorie-wise it will be about the same as a McDonald's small. I decide to make that my tentative plan because I can't think of a way to explain ordering McDonald's again—nor when I'll have time to do a fry run between various child pick-ups and dinner. I regret not having eaten fries at lunchtime.

My kids are thrilled. They love the frozen fries and don't even complain that we are having eggs for dinner, acting like eggs and fries is the most normal meal in the world. I split the fries up almost evenly, leaving a little more for the kids, but keeping a reasonable amount for myself, and we eat them together. While we are eating it occurs to me that I don't know that I've ever eaten fries with my kids. I wonder if they notice (or if they'd prefer that I leave all the fries for them). I'm a little amazed at how lovely and normal it feels. I want them to know that moms—that grown-up women—eat fries.

We finish together and go upstairs so the kids can have showers and tantrums, and get ready for bed. I'm not happy about how my body feels, or looks, or about the anxiety that keeps trying to push its way to the surface, but still I feel something that reminds me a lot of happiness.

Reflections

I'm not not-afraid of fries. In fact, Emily has asked me to follow up with a different size or brand of fries this week, to build on last week's Frypalooza (trademark pending), and I'm really anxious about it. Though if this past week has taught me anything, it's that I can do the hardest, scariest things and survive. And that if I'm lucky, those things might lead to glimmers of normalcy that make it all feel worth it.

CHAPTER 71

Top Five Reasons I'm Thrilled I Didn't Have to Go for a Long Walk Today

5. It's not very nice out.
4. I'm tired and don't feel amazing.
3. This weather is hell on my hair.
2. I have so much stuff to do.
1. This feels like progress, and a relief. The ED isn't the boss of me.

CHAPTER 72

When my dad was a kid, he and his sisters hated chocolate and all things sweet. His mother, my grandmother, loved marshmallow chocolate cookies (called Whippets, for anyone in the know). Because she didn't want to be the only one eating them in her house, she would pay her children fifteen cents for every cookie they ate (that's completely normal, right?). And legend has it that my dad and my aunts would take the cash, toss the cookies, and pool their money together whenever the bag got low, replacing it with a brand-new bag (which cost forty-five cents). Unbeknownst to my grandmother, she would pay them to eat cookies from a bottomless bag for years.

Thirty-five years after that, my dad would be sitting in a vacation home with his self-proclaimed "chocoholic" wife and eleven-year-old daughter, watching said daughter cram chocolate cookies into her mouth. And he'd bet both his wife and his daughter they couldn't stop eating chocolate for a year.

He said that if my mom could do it, he'd buy her a mink coat (gross. I know. Please address all complaints to my parents) and if I could do it, he'd give me fifty dollars ($112 in today's money for anyone else who was hoping that it would be closer to $1000). We obviously accepted.

The rules were zero chocolate things. Nothing chocolate-flavored (like those cheap Easter eggs made with oil and cocoa and tears), nothing carob (for people who didn't grow up in the early eighties, carob was a "healthier" chocolate substitute that a 2018 *New Yorker* piece credits for having "*traumatized a generation*"). There was to be zero chocolate anything, not even chocolate-flavored lip balm (an actual thing, look it up).

We both succeeded. As you can imagine, I got a lot of attention for my incredible self-control. As you probably can't imagine I didn't make the connection between this chocolate bet and all the praise and the self-denial and my eating disorder, until approximately a week ago.

I didn't cheat. Not once. I spoke about my year of no-chocolate at the board finals of the school public speaking competition (I always represented my school at the board finals, but never won. Funny speeches never won and that was all I knew how to do, even then). My line at parties (and by *parties*, I mean birthday parties, when I was telling someone's surprised mother that I couldn't have any cake) was that it was the year I discovered butterscotch, but really, it was the year I discovered how much power lay in my ability to deny myself things most people wanted.

At the end of the year, my mom and I had a big chocolate party attended by all of our friends, and I got my fifty dollars and my mom got her wearable dead animal. After a few weeks of panicking every time I bit into a chocolate bar (I'd forget the bet was over) and stress dreams about cheating on the bet, or losing the bet, things went back to normal.

And then six months later, we would travel to Grenada, and a client of my dad's would refer to me as "hefty," my parents would agree, and I would never be the same. I'd skip breakfast the next morning, and I wouldn't eat cake again for just over thirty-five years.

The praise I got when I started restricting was even shinier and more sparkly than the praise I got during the chocolate bet. Because when I stopped eating chocolate for the bet, I was still eating other calorically dense foods, and I was still chubby. When I stopped eating chocolate because I wanted to change my body, I was on a *self-improvement journey.* The praise that time around wasn't only for the way I acted; it was also for what I was doing for myself, and within about a month, it was for the way I looked.

So it made a lot of sense that I thought my self-control made me special. And that smallness made me special—more special than anything else I could offer.

I'd hear people talking about their inability to get to the gym or inability to resist certain foods and I'd feel a little superior. This would never be my problem.

I'd hear about people with sections of their closets filled with clothing that no longer fit. This would never be my problem.

Friends would compliment me on my body, store clerks would compliment me on my body, strangers would compliment me on my body. I remember two girls coming up to me at the university gym and asking how I got my "six pack" (I guess my abs had been visible under my sweaty tank top). What I should have said was, "This is my second time here today. I have a six-pack because I don't have enough body fat, I don't get a period, and my bone density is a disaster," but instead, I got on the ground and showed them how to do a crunch.

At some point, there was a shift. I recognized that I had to hide the amount of time I spent exercising and the number of foods I didn't eat, but the body compliments persisted. The only time I wasn't getting compliments on my appearance was when I hit absolute rock bottom in grade eleven, and those compliments started right back up again as soon as I was discharged from the hospital at what I now recognize was a ludicrously low body weight. For the first year we were friends, Kirsten was convinced that I ate chocolate for breakfast and all day long (because of things I said, and things I posted on social media, and an article I'd written in a parenting magazine). Cali thought I never exercised and snacked constantly (because of things I said, and things I posted on social media, and an article I'd written in a parenting magazine). People knew I walked a lot, but that also generally garnered even more praise (*I wish I could walk as much as you do!*). Though once in a while I'd bump into someone in an area far enough from my house and they'd see a sleeping child in my stroller and say, "how did you get here? You didn't walk, did you?" which was always a harsh—if fleeting—reminder that things were not okay. At a certain point I recognized that my actions weren't impressive or praise-worthy, but I still had a lot wrapped up in continuing to do them, because they kept my body tiny.

When I started this recovery effort, I was worried people would think that I'd lost my ability to control, well, everything. This was something everyone knew I was good at! Did I want them to think that I'd just ... let myself go? Was I prepared to trade all that admiration for pity?

Letting oneself go is a turn of phrase I'm very familiar with. "*She let herself go*," my mom would say about a neighbor or friend whose body had changed. She would say it with sympathy or amusement or a combination of both. As if this were the worst possible transgression. As though by no longer putting her appearance first, this woman, mother, friend, human had stopped caring about herself. And that's what I used to think too, that's what I had been *conditioned* to think.

I used to think there was nothing more important than being in control of my body and what I ate and how I looked, at all times. I've spent my life making sure that no one would ever think I let myself go. But as I've started to let go (of numbers, of judgment, of fear, of guilt, of unrelenting self-criticism and second guessing, of old ideas about what makes me valuable, or acceptable, of the idea that being more free and more open and less regimented is somehow bad, or wrong), I've realized that letting go is the answer.

Letting go is allowing me to be more vulnerable, more honest, more relaxed, more accepting, more forgiving. It's allowing me to see just how sad it is to believe that denying yourself things like food and rest make you more valuable.

The key to being happy isn't restricting yourself into as tiny a body and life as possible. Or fitting into the tiniest size. People who value those things above everything else are stuck in diet culture. They don't have the answers, they are broken too.

Not long ago, I heard a story about a mother who criticizes her adult daughter's body to her face. And while my first reaction was fury—this is the mother of an amazing, hilarious, kind, beautiful, brilliant woman whom any mother would be so thrilled to have birthed—I also felt sad for her. If smallness is really what this mother values to the extent that she's willing to hurt her own child—to the extent that she is unable to really *see* her own child—she is missing everything.

Letting go has actually been my goal all along, I just had to let go enough to see that.

CHAPTER 73

I recently had a decorator in my house (you would understand if you could see my ugly chandelier and matching sconces), and just before she left, three minutes before I had to be on a call, she mentioned that her fourteen-year-old had recently been hospitalized for anorexia (in the context of a discussion about our respective kids, she didn't know anything about me except that I have no sense of spatial reasoning nor what looks nice in a room). And—even though I *never* do this—I told her that I too had been hospitalized for anorexia at age fourteen and that she should reach out if she wanted to, that I'd be happy to talk to her, or her daughter. And then I ran up to take my call with shaking hands. Because opening up to strangers—even strangers who I want to be open with—still feels stressful in a way I can't describe.

The decorator hasn't reached out yet, but since then I've been thinking about whether there is anything I could say to her daughter that would make a difference. Or if there was anything I could have said to fourteen-year-old me.

When I was fourteen, I sat down with a well-meaning adult. She had recovered from anorexia as had her niece. Her other niece and her sister had been chronically ill with it for many years (genetics!) and she didn't think her sister was going to live much longer.

I don't know how this talk came to be, but her plan was to talk me out of it. And my plan was to completely ignore her.

Not to be all braggy, but guess whose plan worked out?

I don't know why I even agreed to that talk. Not only was I uninterested in anything she had to say, I was pretty enamored with anorexia at that point. It was giving me everything it was supposed to. I got compliments all the time for how pretty and tiny I was and I got just the right amount of attention ("you have so much self-control!"). I was as numb as I needed to be, I still had lots of energy (adrenaline!), and my not-eating infuriated my parents. I had no intention of changing anything. Anorexia and I were still in the honeymoon phase.

Which is why I'm not sure I could say anything that would make a difference to someone in that place. I'm not even sure there's anything I could say to fourteen-year-old me that would have made a difference (which checks out. Why would I start being nice to myself all of a sudden, even to the grown-up version?)

So what on earth would I say? It's like trying to get through to a cult member. Though, sometimes people leave cults. Maybe it would make more sense to write a letter. I remember feeling like I was being lectured by an annoying adult-know-it-all and zoning out. It's harder to zone out when you're reading a letter. And you can get a letter back from the trash (or your trash folder) and reread a letter as many times as you need. I think this is the type of thing you might need to read a whole bunch of times, presuming it makes it out of the trash.

Also, I don't want a fourteen-year-old looking me in the eye while thinking that I'm an annoying adult-know-it-all. Teenagers can be mean, especially hungry ones.

Dear fourteen-year-old,

I know that you feel like anorexia is part of your identity. It's not. It's an illness.

Anorexia doesn't make you special or worthy. You are special and worthy because you are a person who exists in the world.

What feels like admiration from the people around you is probably sadness. And even if it's not, in this fucked-up diet-culture society, the people who admire your self-control, and your thinness, still get to live their whole lives. Their admiration is fleeting, and they wouldn't trade places with you for anything. They aren't missing shared meals and experiences to stay in a small body. They understand that's not a fair trade.

People (your parents, or your friends) might be paying more attention on account of your illness and that might make you feel cared for. But you are just as cared for when you aren't ill. All you have to do is ask. You don't have to make your outsides match your insides. When you tell people who love you that you are struggling, they will believe you. No proof required. You don't have to keep hurting yourself to feel loved, I promise.

Right now, it feels like a drug. You can numb out all of your problems and focus all that energy into restriction, but that numbness actually means you're missing your life. And the more numb you get, the less you realize what you're missing.

And if this keeps up, you are going to miss *everything*.

You won't grow out of it. The longer you let it squat in your brain and body, the stronger it will become. Right now it's early days. You can get your life back. It's much harder to rewire neural pathways once they become entrenched. Two years will become ten. And ten will become thirty. And recovery will be so much harder, because you won't remember a version of yourself that wasn't ill.

I know that you think that you have it under control. But you don't. It's a boulder on the steep edge of a mountain.

Maybe you feel like smallness is part of your identity, but it doesn't have to be. You are so much more than your body. Your illness wants you to believe that keeping your body small is more important than freedom. It's a lie.

You deserve your whole life. Don't waste this (I'm serious, you stubborn little fucker. I know you think you know better than I do, but you don't).

I missed a lot of my life. And I didn't notice. Friends, education, careers, jobs, romantic partners were all chosen to accommodate my illness.

I missed trips, ignored ambitions, ruined friendships, and neglected people I love. I lost years that I will never get back.

And I was one of the lucky ones. I didn't die of a heart attack, or drop out of school, or isolate myself in the way a lot of people with our illness do. I was so, so lucky and I still feel like I'm going to drown in a sea of regret when I think about all of the sacrifices I made at the altar of anorexia.

Don't wait thirty years to see what you missed. You might not even get thirty years. Don't miss your one precious life.

Love,
Me.

CHAPTER 74

I met someone who we will call Allison (because that's not her real name), in an online recovery community for adults. I joined this community after accepting that my weight loss and inability to eat most things meant I still had an eating disorder, but before I was convinced I wanted to recover.

While I lurked in the online space hoping to absorb other people's bravery by osmosis (I know. Ridiculous. That only works in person), Allison posted with regularity.

And then one day I posted something (who knows what), and she private messaged me to say she really identified with whatever I'd written, and did I want to exchange email addresses—you aren't allowed to DM in that community, because everything is supposed to be very transparent (for example, the fact that even adults can't be trusted to message each other). I said yes, and for the next few months we got to know each other through a flurry of novella-length emails—picture online dating, but with no expectation of romance or meeting anytime soon (we live on different continents). We had so much in common—from the age of onset of anorexia, to what triggered our relapses (breastfeeding our youngest child); pregnancies (we were both eleven weeks pregnant at our weddings, had used clomid to get pregnant, and had given birth to tiny babies); family stories (we were both born to save our deeply depressed grandmothers after car accidents had taken someone they loved, in my case my grandfather), very pale, very bald husbands; etc., etc., etc. It was a little eerie. And most importantly, for the first time since I was a teenager, I had a friend who understood what it was like to live with an eating disorder, and who also understood how hard it was to try to recover as an adult, and as a mother.

At first it was amazing. We wanted the same things from our recoveries, and had similar fear foods, exercise compulsions, and aspirations. The problem was that because we were so similar in so many ways, our recoveries started blurring together.

When she read a very popular diet book her dentist recommended (that's fine! People in recovery from restrictive eating disorders read diet books all. the. time!) and freaked out about it, I talked her down, but to do so, I had to listen to her tell me why she was suddenly afraid of carbs (something that had never really bothered me because I had one of those retro eating disorders that started when dietary fat was scary, and carbs were fine). Not shockingly, all the talking about the things that scared her, and why they scared her, made me secretly wonder if she was right and if we should both be afraid. It took me a long time to shake that off.

About eighteen months into our online friendship, she came to visit with her husband and kids (who were similar to mine in age and temperament). And although this hadn't been the case when we planned the visit, she was in the midst of a full relapse. I wasn't particularly concerned about how her relapse would affect me when she arrived because I was in a pretty good place. But spending two weeks with someone who is afraid of everything I'd worked so hard to no longer be afraid of was harder than I expected. I didn't have the bandwidth to talk back to her eating disorder and my own at the same time (if you are a parent, imagine two of your children yelling at you, one in each ear. If you aren't a parent, imagine two shrill, screeching hyenas screeching at you, one in each ear). There wasn't any space to hear my own thoughts—the eating disorder chatter was deafening.

We talked about recovery a lot more than I wanted, or expected. And although on that visit she was very keen to get back on track, like anyone in a relapse, she struggled with negative thoughts. The problem was that my recovery was still too new for me not to find them persuasive when she said them out loud. When she told me that full recovery was impossible for people "like us" (and I don't think she meant long-haired brunettes born in February), and that everyone we knew from the recovery forum—which I'd left but she was now moderating—was either fat and miserable, fat and miserable and on their way to a relapse, or miserable and relapsing, my conviction started to waver.

When she said there's no such thing as full recovery, and that *every single one* of the people I believed to be fully recovered was not fully recovered, I started to lose hope. And when a few months after her visit she told me she was finding balance and happiness with light macro counting and a couple days a week of CrossFit (to me, the cultiest, weirdest of all the workouts), I wondered if she had the best of both worlds.

Of course, she wasn't getting the best of anything. She had decided to stay in quasi-recovery and was trying to rationalize her choices by convincing me it was the only option that made sense. And I was nearly convinced.

Because we had both been ill for the same amount of time, I thought if she declared that it was too late for her, it was too late for me. When she announced that her life was perfectly good in quasi-recovery, I started to think that mine was as good as it could get. And when she decided that full recovery wasn't possible for her, I understood "for us."

Eating disorders are very comparative by nature. A rest day is made infinitely harder when my husband goes for a walk, or if a friend mentions her Peloton workout, or if I see that an acquaintance on Instagram has gone for a long run (or if I drive by someone on the street in workout attire who looks a little sweaty). I don't know why that is. Why is it that knowing that other people—whose bodies are obviously in no way connected to my body—have exercised makes the act of being still so much harder? I suspect that it boils down to a lack of confidence. It's hard to completely trust that I'm doing the right thing all the time. And I take what other people do or don't do and eat or don't eat as evidence of what normal is, and how things are supposed to work—especially if whatever they are doing seems to be working for them. But it's pretty hard to know what's working for someone unless you are them. And even if I were to establish that whatever someone else is doing is bringing them the optimal level of happiness and health, that might not be what works for me. Right now, the thing that's working for me is doing all the things I need to do to recover, like not exercising. I can't settle into equilibrium without spending some time at the other extreme, as much as I wish that I could.

I can't decide if the comparison with Allison and her recovery comes from the same place as the extra stress I feel being still when I know that people around me are exercising. It's probably a little more complicated than that. Recovery involves taking a giant leap of faith—it makes sense that we look for others who have similar histories and have succeeded. Success stories are inspiring and comforting, and other people's failures can feel so incredibly personal. When Allison made the decision to stay in quasi-recovery, it felt like a warning. It didn't cross my mind that I was confusing relief with happiness, settling with comfort, fear with dogma.

I kept thinking that if this person whose illness was more like mine than anyone else's has decided that it was pointless, didn't that apply to me too? I failed to take into account that our personalities are completely different (Kirsten spent twenty minutes talking to Allison at the park, pulled me aside, and said, "you are *nothing alike*. I don't know why you think that you are the same").

And Kirsten was right (Oh, god. How many times have I said that in this book? She can never read any of this). But for our illnesses, histories, and some superficial similarities, Allison and I aren't alike at all. And even if we were the same, even if we were identical twins separated at birth, we didn't have to share the same fate. No two people are exactly the same, and all our recoveries are as unique as we are.

I'd like to say that I learned from this experience immediately, because that's the kind of evolved, self-aware person that I am, but obviously I can't, because I'm not. Not that many months after I made peace with (almost) everything that had gone down with Allison, I started a recovery account on Instagram and accidentally made some friends (despite a great deal of apprehension about internet friends at this point). One of those friends had recovered from a longstanding eating disorder and exercise addiction, which gave me a lot of hope (and occasionally made me feel like a giant loser because of how much quicker she'd been able to recover than I had). And then she relapsed and didn't tell me. When she did eventually tell me, it became apparent she'd been struggling for months, and that she was never as recovered as she'd made herself out to be. She is working hard to get her recovery back on track but has made it clear she doesn't necessarily aspire to be fully recovered. She thinks harm reduction is a sufficient goal for many people, and that most people don't fully recover. And learning this was initially incredibly destabilizing, and in some moments devastating. How many times do I have to learn the same fucking lesson?

Of course, the lesson is that other people's recoveries or feelings about recovery can't be allowed to change my goals, or how I feel about my own recovery. If someone struggling with addiction to drugs or alcohol were to tell me they didn't believe in full recovery from substances, I'd understand that's what they need to believe right now, because their addiction still has a firm grip on them. I wouldn't stop believing that people can recover from addiction. Frustration and fear and despair are common human emotions. That doesn't mean there aren't people who have persevered and succeeded.

Just like I'm not suddenly lazier than I was before I heard about my friend's long run today, I'm no less capable of recovery because some people don't believe in it for themselves. Maybe they will change their minds one day and they aren't quite there yet. And maybe they need me to go first and prove to them that full recovery exists. And maybe, we are simply destined to take different paths.

CHAPTER 75

Never Have I Ever

~~Ordered something off a menu just because I thought it might taste good~~

~~Gone a whole day without knowing how many calories I'd consumed~~

~~Spent a whole day in my pyjamas~~

~~Stayed home on a snowy or rainy weekend~~

~~Stopped eating just because I was full~~

~~Not known the exact distance between my thighs~~

~~Had an entire day where the thought "you are so fat" didn't go through my head~~

Watched a show about the Kardashians

CHAPTER 76

I started counting calories on a Monday in grade seven. My health teacher (who was also my French teacher, social studies teacher, and phys ed teacher) handed out a few sheets of paper listing common foods and their caloric values and told us to tally up our calories from the day before. The sheet of paper also had ranges for what is ideal (weight maintenance) and what is too much (weight gain) and what is too little (weight loss). I was elated to see my caloric intake from the day before fell into the too-little zone (weirdly I can still remember the exact number of calories I landed on that day, despite not being able to remember why I opened Google ten minutes ago). I'd already been restricting food for many months, but suddenly I had at my disposal a way to measure everything. And that was how the number of calories I'd consumed on that random Sunday became my first caloric maximum (these would get increasingly lower as my illness progressed).

Because the internet didn't exist back then, I had to use calorie books. These were like dictionaries (because the internet didn't exist back then, I also had to use dictionaries) with foods and their caloric values listed in alphabetical order. I had three calorie books at the beginning (for cross referencing purposes—if in doubt I'd always choose the highest value), two were pocket-sized, and I'd keep them in my actual pockets, and one was a bigger, heavier one I'd usually read for fun at home, picking things to add to my mental list of foods I'd never eat. It didn't take long for me to memorize just about everything (this explains why I have no room left in my head for anything important). Calories started taking up a lot of real estate in my brain—I'd add and re-add the numbers over and over, and I counted absolutely everything. Piece of gum? Five calories. Diet pop? Three calories. Diet Jell-o? Thirty-six calories. Ice water? Freebie! (Wait! Had someone added a slice of lemon?)

Not long ago, my parents gave me back the contents of my childhood closet, and I went through old notebooks to refresh my memory on important things I'd learned, like mitosis and how to diagram a sentence. I was struck by how nice my handwriting used to be, how many cartoon dogs I used to draw, and the fact that every margin on every page in every book had little columns of numbers on it. I used to have to write those numbers down so I could stop adding them up in my head and pay attention in class. Sometimes, I'd have to do it multiple times in the same class. This behavior continued throughout university and law school and even into my working life, as a lawyer at the Department of Justice.

I've blamed calorie counting for a lot of my illness. When my parents took away the bathroom scale, and I had no idea if I was gaining or losing weight, I handled that by further reducing my caloric intake (this caused some pretty significant weight loss, and I wound up in the hospital for the second time in two months. Zero stars). I've felt extreme guilt and panic throughout this recovery effort when I thought I was going beyond my limit at a particular meal or when I didn't have a precise number to land on. But I couldn't stop counting. The numbers were my worst enemy (along with people who drive really slow in the fast lane and condescending teenagers who work at Sephora), but I couldn't let them go.

One day earlier this year Emily asked me to tell her my caloric maximums for every meal and snack. These have obviously gotten higher over the years and certainly over the course of my recovery, but

I was still embarrassed by this question (*this is my line in the sand?*). I knew that she knew that even though I'd stopped measuring and weighing things, I was still counting with a fair degree of precision, but saying it out loud made me feel like a failure. Though I told her, and from that day forward we worked to turn those maximums into minimums. This was obviously hard and stressful and didn't happen immediately, but it was my first step toward stopping. Because as the numbers got higher, more things fit into my allotments. I could eat things that were harder to count with less stress.

The real turning point came a few weeks ago when I went to visit Kirsten and Kevin and Neil (they have now all moved away to the same city and claim it has nothing to do with me. Please look for my next book titled *Everyone I Love Keeps Moving Away. This Book Has No Funny Parts*). I hadn't gone with the intention of stopping calorie counting, but I had gone with strict instructions from Emily not to order any modifications (like dressing on the side) and to act like someone who is easygoing around food (upon hearing the plan Kirsten promptly introduced the hashtag #easygoing).

We had a lot of scary, boozy restaurant meals over the course of the weekend (I only cried once and was only outrageously angry at Kirsten for about ten minutes. So much progress!). Toward the end of my first day, I noticed I hadn't tallied anything up for the first time since that fateful day in the seventh grade. I decided to keep it up as long as I could. Kevin was about sixty percent less mocky than Kirsten and also fully on board with operation #easygoing ("An easygoing person would have ordered by now!," "An easygoing person would have a bite of my vegan crème brûlée," "An easygoing person would have some of my chips and salsa"), and the streak continued.

Many people view calorie counting as harmless or even helpful. Calorie counts are on more and more menus and packages, and the people behind this (like my brother-in-law, who was a very loud voice in favor, including at a Senate Committee hearing on the subject) claim that knowledge is power. But I don't believe this to be true. The problem with calorie counting, in addition to the fact that it reduces food to numbers and takes away all or most of the enjoyment, is that it messes around with your natural hunger cues. One of the hardest things for me to change has been trying to decide if I want a snack or a glass of wine without tallying up my daily intake to see if there's room in my caloric budget. That's how I've always known when to stop eating, and what and how much to eat.

For people stuck in diet culture, it's no better. It leads to feelings of food dissatisfaction and often bingeing or "failed" diets. If we let ourselves eat to satiety, and listen to our bodies, things work the way they should. If food is reduced to a number, we lose the ability to listen to our hunger cues and cravings. The lowest calorie food is often not what we need. Calories are simply units of energy and don't give the full picture.

I've heard people in late stages of recovery say they still count calories to make sure they have eaten enough. Though if you have been in recovery for a while, you generally know if you have eaten enough, and you know if you are restricting. Calorie counting is tedious and joy-sucking at best and dangerous and life-destroying at its worst. Yet giving it up has been one of the hardest things I've ever done.

It's been nearly four weeks since I stopped counting. This isn't to say that it's easy or natural yet. I still have urges to add everything up. The impulse is loud and persistent, like a mosquito bite begging to be itched. And sometimes I still count automatically and have to stop myself, usually by making the next meal something with small components that are harder to add up effortlessly.

Like with all other recovery things, my progress hasn't been completely linear. Some days are pretty easy, and others are frustratingly, mind-numbingly difficult.

But so far, for the most part, I'm doing it. And I'm amazed. Every day feels a tiny bit easier, and it has been rewarding in all the important ways. I've been able to eat things I would have said no to previously, I've been slightly more present (admittedly a very low bar) at meals, I've been able to say yes to after-dinner wine, and weird marinated things in a salad bar, and a slice of cake on my son's birthday. It has given me this glimpse of everything I've been working toward, and it has given me hope.

I've been thinking a lot about why it was suddenly possible to stop counting calories on that weekend away. I think it boils down to a lot of the predictable things I've already mentioned—eating less countable and more unfamiliar foods, distracting myself when numbers pop into my head, months of working to turn my previous caloric maximums into minimums. Also, I think it's the weight gain. I think that it's made the noise a little easier to ignore. It's made the eating disorder thoughts a little less invasive, and it's given me more flexibility.

Weight gain has felt like the worst, scariest thing so many times over the course of my recovery, but I think it's the thing that ultimately changed everything. Even how I feel about weight gain.

CHAPTER 77

When I started writing this book, I thought I'd either stop writing (say, if I quit recovery) or that it would end with a neat bow. I'd wake up one day, and the birds would be chirping, and the sun would be shining, and I'd be in the mood for a giant stack of chocolate chip pancakes—no looking back.

But that's not what happened. Recovery isn't linear, and sometimes progress is very slow. And sometimes it's nearly imperceptible.

Last month Emily and I had a long talk. I'd been feeling discouraged because things that should feel easy or enjoyable often still feel so hard. And I asked her if maybe I'm just broken because I've been at this for so long and it's all so much work, and it never occurred to me that I'm supposed to be enjoying anything (did anyone else know fries are supposed to be eaten warm?). We decided to keep going, and we put some plans in place, but the whole thing was pretty depressing.

Then later that same day I thought about a dinner I'd gone to the previous night. And it occurred to me that I'd ordered a cocktail because I *wanted one*. I had a salad with halloumi (fried cheese!) in it, and it hadn't crossed my mind to order it without the halloumi, even though it made calorie counting with any precision nearly impossible. Our bread came buttered, and not only did I not send it back, I ate some. My friend and I both had the same main course, only she didn't finish hers ("This is too much! I'm so full!") but

I finished mine. And while admittedly it wasn't the world's most challenging meal, these things were beyond my contemplation even a few months ago.

And that weekend, I went out of town. I went out for lunches and brunches and dinners, which all started with cocktails and shared appetizers and ended with wine and laughter. I spent hours sitting around talking to my closest friends and wasn't consumed with the thought that I should be moving, or that we should be walking. I was engaged and grateful and delighted to be with people I love and who love me back (and who laugh at my jokes).

I decided that I'd try not to tally up my daily calories while I was away, and now I'm home, and it's been five weeks since I've gone to bed knowing how many calories I've consumed in any given day. It isn't easy yet: the ED thrusts numbers at me constantly and forcefully, but for the first time I have the strength to ignore them.

I thought for the longest time that this weight (just about my day hospital goal weight) was something I could never learn to live with. And now, I feel mostly okay in my body most of the time. I'm still nervous about gaining, but experience has taught me that I'm more resilient than I knew, and that I can deal with whatever happens next.

I used to worry that by giving up my ED, I'd be losing more than I had to gain (this pun is amazing, I'm leaving it). I didn't feel ready to give up my small body and the compliments and the feeling of being excellent at something other people struggle with. I didn't want to lose the feeling of being in complete control. Though I've come to realize the control is a prison. It's so much more meaningful to be comfortable in your own skin. There is nothing special about being a person who spends their whole life trying to be smaller. But to be someone who can find pleasure in food and rest, who can be their whole, unapologetic self and live their whole unrestricted, messy life is miraculous. Recovery can be miraculous.

You don't wake up recovered one day. These little pinpricks of light come in and illuminate dark places so gradually that it's sometimes impossible to notice—but then, one day you look around and there's light where there once wasn't.

My world is a little brighter every day.

CHAPTER 78

May 25, 2021

<u>To Do, 5.0</u>

- Keep working on the fear foods list, don't get complacent
- Try new things (even if they aren't on the list because you were unaware of their existence)
- Keep doing all the rest days, even when the weather is amazing and all you want is a walk. One day you will be ready to listen to your gut when it comes to these things, but not quite yet.
- Keep doing yoga
- Get rid of your old tiny clothes, you don't need them anymore
- Know that there are still going to be hard days, know that they will pass
- Know that there are still going to be days when you hate this body, know that they will pass
- Appreciate how very far you've come
- Do the things that scare you
- Pretend you aren't terrified
- Know that it's going to be okay
- Breathe

ACKNOWLEDGEMENTS

It's hard not to make this an eleven-page essay—I have so many wonderful friends (and very few crappy ones). So first off, a blanket thank you to all my friends (unless you are one of the crappy ones, you know who you are).

Thank you to my little writing group—Elspeth, Pascale, and Sarah—for being the most supportive one anyone could ask for. Thank you for the motivation and the kindness and the reassurance and the laughs.

Pascale and Elspeth, thank you for always answering every ridiculous text beginning with "what do you think of this...?" or "does this work?" or "does this make sense to you?" or "would you please give this a quick read?" You are both so amazing (and good at so many things that it's a little disconcerting).

Speaking of things you're so good at, Elspeth, thank you for the beautiful cover design. I think it's a little weird that you are this talented at everything and as nice as you are. If I was as good at as many things as you, I'd be insufferable.

Thank you, Rebecca, for all you do for women writers, and for believing in this book, and me, and for always laughing at my jokes.

Thank you, Val, for your very keen eye, excellent advice, and absolute loveliness.

Thank you, Kevin and Neil, for your general awesomeness, and for always being there when it matters.

Thank you, Joanne, for being the most fabulous sounding board and such a thoughtful early reader and for allowing me to believe that other people might want to read this book, even when I wasn't sure it should be read by anyone.

Sara, you are another early reader whose enthusiasm, encouragement and unlimited supply of kindness has been invaluable, thank you.

Thank you, Alix, for frequently being the voice of reason and such a generous, supportive friend, and for reading this book more times than anyone, including me.

Thank you, Kier, for a list of things far too long to enumerate. I'm so grateful.

Thank you, Emily, for the patience, insight, and generosity that led to so many things that have changed my life.

Thank you, Kirsten, for the late nights, teary meals, ridiculous arguments, uncontrollable laughter, unceasing encouragement, and endless fun—and for being the actual best.

Thank you to my parents for doing the best you could in an impossibly difficult situation that I'm sure left you feeling overwhelmed and powerless much of the time. The way we talk about food and bodies has changed a lot in the last few decades, and we are all still learning. I know and appreciate that you've always wanted the best for me.

Thank you, Jacob, for your unwavering support with my recovery and this project and basically everything else I've ever wanted to do. I'm so lucky. I love you.

And finally, thank you to my kids for giving me so many reasons to want more and every reason to keep going. You are everything.